Camus's Rebellious Thought

Camus's Rebellious Thought

V. John Bachman

Talus Titles
Van Schaick Island, New York
1998

Copyright 1998
V. John Bachman

Library of Congress Catalog Card Number 98-90608

ISBN 0-9666421-0-4

Printed in the United States of America

pour Dolly

amante de francais
et de moi
et ma bien-aimée

Contents

Acknowledgments vii

Preface ix

Chapters
   I   Solidarity and Rebellion 1

   II   Contraries and Contradictions 17

   III   Absurd Beginnings 37

   IV   Remnants and Rebels 61

   V   Portrait of Rebellion 87

   VI   Gentle Vision and Vehement Irony 107

   VII   The Rebellious Stance 125

Bibliography 139

Acknowledgments

The full richness of Albert Camus's thought can only be gained by repeated conversation with the whole of his works. Here, I have chosen to focus on his philosophic and creative works and on the mode of thought first manifested in the earliest stage of his writing.

The uncanny insight of Professor Helen W. Schrader, of Stanford University, led to my long acquaintance with Albert Camus. Since I first savored his work, my enthusiasm has not waned. For her introduction and enduring interest in Camus studies I express my continuing gratitude to Professor Schrader.

During this long exploration, from the very beginning, my intimate sustainer, Dolly Kissling Bachman, with her presence and advice, has contributed immeasurably to the surveying of this bountiful land.

* * * * *

Permissions to include quotations from their publications have been kindly granted by publishing houses indicated:

Chapter I: *Alger-Républicain*, May-June, 1939; *Soir-Républicain*, October-December, 1939; Herbert R. Lottman, *Albert Camus*, George Braziller, New York, 1980; Olivier Todd, *Albert Camus, a Life*, Benjamin Ivry, translator, Knopf, New York, 1997, p. 80.

Chapter II: Albert Camus, *Essais*, Roger Quilliot et Louis Faucon, annotateurs, Gallimard et Calmann-Lévy, Paris, 1965, pp. 6, 19-22, 35, 37, 39, 44, 47-50, my translations.

Chapter III: Jean-Paul Sartre, "Explication de L'Étranger," *Situation* I (Gallimard, Paris, 1947); Albert Camus, *Théâtre, Récits, Nouvelles*, Roger Quilliot, annotateur, Éditions Gallimard, Paris, 1962, p. 1737; Albert Camus, *The Stranger*, Stuart Gilbert, translator, Vintage, New York, 1946, p. 72; Albert Camus, *The Myth of Sisyphus*, Justin O'Brien, translator, Vintage, New York, 1955; Albert Camus, *Caligula and Three Other Plays*, Stuart Gilbert, translator, Vintage, New York, 1958, pp. 51-52; Albert Camus, *Lyrical and Critical Essays*, Philip Thody, editor, Ellen Conroy Kennedy, translator, Vintage, New York, 1970, pp. 159, 356; Todd, *Albert Camus*, pp. 130, 133.

Chapter IV: *Théâtre, Récits, Nouvelles*, p. 1423; *Caligula and Three Other Plays*, p. viii.

Chapter V: *The Myth of Sisyphus*, Justin O'Brien, translator, Vintage, New York, 1955, p. 90; Albert Camus, *The Rebel*, Anthony Bower, translator, Vintage, New York, 1956, pp. 173, 304, 306.

Otherwise, all cited references are indirect.

Preface

In 1957 Albert Camus was awarded the Nobel Prize for Literature, the citation noting "his important literary production, which with clear-sighted earnestness illuminated the problems of the human conscience in our times."

From his birthplace in Mondovi, Algeria, to his burial place in Lourmarin, France—and the many places between—I have visited sites associated with Albert Camus. Decades of interest are antecedent to this book, for his thought has intrigued me from the moment I was introduced.

My interest sometimes surprises me, for I am not as free of constraints as was he. And I'm not sure I would have responded well to the man Camus. But this is not a book about Camus, the man. There are two voluminous biographies of Albert Camus, the man. This book is about Albert Camus, the writer.

Albert Camus, the writer, was many things—journalist, essayist, dramatist, novelist, moralist.

He wrote about existentialism, since it was widely current at the time. And Americans, even educated Americans, persist in tagging him as an "existentialist," though he repeatedly said that he was not.

Many learned of Camus through his first novel, *The Stranger*, where he wrote of the absurd. And many persist in confining him to the absurd.

In a previous study of Camus's non-fiction writings, I presented counter-valence as Camus's implicit mode in controversial discourse. That counter-valence was directed from the middle and applied to each of the opposing antagonists. Camus's little essay, "Between Yes and No," although speaking of other things, resonates with counter-valence.

"Between-ness" also characterizes the thought found in his philosophic and creative writings. One constant, tacit motif is embedded in them: that of rebellion. Rebellious thought, sometimes implicit, but often explicit, is the dominant feature of Camus's creative work. His practice as a writer is clearly discerned through the lens of rebellion—rebellion as he defined it.

This book mainly considers Camus's philosophic and creative works, although his early journalism is also examined. In the book I offer what I've discovered in the legacy of rebellious thought bequeathed by Camus.

I

Solidarity and Rebellion

Events of the 1990s have confirmed Albert Camus's insights of years before. He had criticized Russian Communism severely in the 1950s. Now Russian Communism has fallen.

In the 1950s Camus detailed a great contradiction: though Russian Communism asserted to be for the workers and the people, it was a repressive, totalitarian system, dominating the people "for their own benefit." Forty years later, Camus's assessment and condemnation have been authenticated by the break-down and dismantling of Communism's Russian/European empire.

In his own time, Camus, a man of the political left, was faulted by his fellows on the left for not being *engagé,* for not "dirtying his hands" in the activities of partisanship, for his refusal to commit himself to a party. He had veered away, they said, from the promise of his beginnings. Indeed, he had moved beyond his beginning—but the "promise" was not made by him. He had not marked out a course; he did not follow a set course. He had no system to develop or fulfill. Critics erred in assuming that Camus was concerned about consistency.

In 1960, the headline,"ABSURD," announced Camus's death.

Death at forty-six was "absurd." And so was the immediate conjecture of many: "Suicide!" Suicide would have fit the reputation for absurdity assigned him. But the surmise was one more instance of the misunderstandings which he suffered. Albert Camus was famous, revered, and misunderstood. His death deprived the world of an artist, of a conscience, of a thinker—and of his paradigmatic alternative to *parti pris*, to ideology, to fixed commitment.

Death by suicide might have silenced his critics. It would have been the proper ending of a career they had called "absurd." They'd identified him with the absurd because he'd begun with it. Though he'd gone beyond his beginnings, his antagonists—and many of the public-at-large—persisted in confining him in those beginnings, even in his death.

Death by suicide? He had raised the question himself in *The Myth of Sisyphus* when he had delineated the absurd and posed the "one philosophical question—that of suicide." But his death was accidental. He was a passenger, not the driver, in a high-performance car which went airborne and crashed into the last of a line of sycamores. In his pocket was the unused train ticket which would have taken him from Provence to Paris. He had accepted the offer of a ride. He had not taken his own life.

Camus never developed consistency, as did Jean Paul Sartre, his most famous associate. It was Camus's inconstancy—his abstention from consistency—which brought on strong disagreement between the two. In 1952, Camus, certainly a man of the left—and a Communist for a brief time—wrote critically of Marxism and Russian Communism in *The Rebel*, a work at odds with the beliefs of the left. Sartre, also a man of the left, and his associates took on the book—and Camus—in severe, sustained attack. The argument was carried on in public, in the pages of papers and journals. In consequence, the two men, formerly close associates, broke apart definitively.

At the time, many thought that Camus lost the argument. Nevertheless, the events of the 1990s, with the exposure of the Communist Party and the great fall of Russian Communism, have exonerated Camus. He had been right in *The Rebel*, far in advance of developments.

Camus was not a party thinker. He was a rebellious thinker, often moving away from a position he had previously articulated. Later work rarely buttressed its predecessors. He was not systematic: he had no system to authenticate. Consistency was of no concern; for Camus began, not with an idea or a schema, but with his sense of compassion, of empathy, of identity with people—especially with the victims of systems and ideologies. The Russian people were among those victims.

The sense of "solidarity"—compelling empathy for others, whether individuals or groups—is a singular characteristic of the man Camus. This trait of solidarity accounts for those stances of his which seemed contradictory to colleagues with whom he generally shared perspective. A man of the left, he was expected to be supportive of the left. But he was as sensitive to victims of the left as to victims of the right. Consequently, he was often as critical of the acts of allies as of those of adversaries.

Solidarity with victims—victims of circumstances, of governments, and of systems—impelled much of Camus's activity. Solidarity and his refusal to follow "lines" made him a rebel in the realms of thought and public expression.

One of Camus's last works, "The Guest," a short story, involves the trait of solidarity. It shows Daru, the protagonist, standing between two cultures—the consequence of his empathy with an Arab charged with murder. He is in the middle—between the French legal system and Arab traditional treatment of murderers.

Daru, a French Algerian, is a school teacher of Arab children in a remote region of Algeria. As a quasi-representative of the French government (before Algerian independence), Daru is a link between the government and the people.

The Arab, accused of murdering his cousin, is left in Daru's charge by a constable who has brought the man to him on the end of a rope. Daru protests when told to walk the man to prison, several miles away. He objects to the treatment of the Arab and to his own assignment. He opposes the application of French law to the Arab, considering it a wrongful imposition. As the constable departs, Daru realizes that the official doubts his national loyalty.

Daru, approving neither the Arab's crime nor the government's actions, shares his private quarters with the man, treating him as a guest, not as a prisoner. He hopes that the culprit will escape to a nomad settlement, where Arab justice will apply.

During the night, the man is given ample opportunity to escape. But the Arab does not slip away.

The next day, the two having walked for some time on the road to the prison, Daru stops at the junction of a pathway and the road. Handing the man some food, specially prepared for the purpose, and a few hundred francs, Daru shows him the pathway which leads to the nomad encampment. The Arab stands there, unmoving. With some impatience, Daru begins his walk back to the schoolhouse. Stopping and looking back from the top of a hill, he is chagrined to see the Arab walking along the way to prison.

Back at the schoolhouse, he enters the classroom and is accosted by scrawled writing on the chalkboard. The words accuse him of handing the Arab over to French justice. He is assailed by the certainty that his students and their families believe that he is responsible for the man's imprisonment. Yet he recognizes that the constable will report the opposite: that Daru's sympathy for the Arab makes him suspect, a non-supporter of

French rule. Both the suspicion of the French and the hostility of the resident Arabs have some validity, but Daru can side with neither party. There is merit and fault on both sides. When, in solidarity with the Arab, he let the prisoner himself decide, Daru was in conflict with both cultures, and in concert with neither.

Daru stood between two alternatives: he could take the Arab to nomad sanctuary, or he could deliver the prisoner to the jail. Gauged by concepts portrayed in *The Rebel*, one act would be that of a revolutionary; the other, the act of a conserver. Daru was neither. He resisted the establishment, but he did not seek ways to displace it. He identified with French culture, but he did not accept unjust actions. He was a rebel.

Written in the midst of the Algerian-French confrontations, the story of Daru is symbolic of Camus's position in that traumatic time. Born and raised in Algeria, yet very much a product of French culture, Camus was not willing to say that one side was right and the other was wrong. He was attacked by people on both sides because, they said, by refusing to join them, he was choosing against them. But alignment with either side would contribute to the endemic violence. For those who choose a side enter into lethal embrace with their opponents. To choose a side would be to license murderous action against people with whom he shared the bonds of solidarity.

Albert Camus was raised in Belcourt, a poor, working class neighborhood in Algiers. He hardly knew his father, who was killed in World War I when Camus was only two. He and his older brother were supported by their mother's work as a domestic, but they were reared, in the same quarters, by their grandmother. Camus grew up in poverty, in the midst of laborers, and lived among the Arabs. There he experienced solidarity, early in life. That was to lead him into intellectual rebellion and into conflict with the establishment.

After gaining a classical education, thanks to the insight and oversight of some discerning teachers (Louis Germain and Jean Grenier, notably), Camus was introduced to the larger world and began his development into his own singularity.

In the mid-1930s, the early years of his manhood, Camus joined the Communist Party. It was an act against bourgeois society. The party seemed to promise a means for improving economic and political conditions for the workers and the Muslims. In the party he was given responsibility for propagandizing and recruiting the Arabs in Algiers. Little is known of his operation in this capacity.

Only a couple of years after joining, Camus left the Communist Party. That, too, was rebellious, rising from his observing the re-direction of the party line. He'd been drawn to the party by its difference from bourgeois conservatism and by its concern for worker and Muslim rights. But when Pierre Laval, leader of the French Communist Party, returned from consultations with the Party in Moscow, he brought new directions for the party line. When the new policies filtered down to Algeria, the local party moved away from support for Muslim nationalist ambitions and those aspirations were no longer supported. This imposition of change, from the top down, was unacceptable for Camus. Party workers had not been consulted, but they were expected to comply.

In his biography of Camus, Herbert Lottman delineates the intra-party fighting of this time. He says that Camus did not resign, but was voted out of the party, and that Camus was not displeased by the action. Whatever the truth of the matter, Camus was never again involved in the Communist Party. He did not go along with the party line.

During this same period, Camus was participating in a theater group, strongly Marxist in orientation, called *Théâtre du Travail* (Theater of Labor). He acted, directed, and wrote for the theater. There, with several others, he wrote his first play, *Révolte dans les Asturies*, dramatizing the struggles of Spanish coal miners in a northwestern province of Spain. As the title indicates, it was a tale of rebellion. After Camus's break with the Communist Party, he and some revolutionary associates who'd also left, continued as a semi-professional company calling itself *Théâtre de l'Équipe* (Theater of the Group).

Camus opposed *parti pris*—the party line—in his experience with the party and in later circumstances. He refused to make a fixed commitment. For the logic of fixed commitment leads to ignoring the virtues of the other position and to affirming nothing but the rightness of your own. Fixed commitment leads to dismissal of an opponent's arguments, out of hand. In extremis, fixed commitment leads to total denial of opposing arguments, to violence—"dirty hands"—to rejection of an opponent's right to be. *Parti pris* violates solidarity.

One of Camus's first significant jobs was as a reporter for *Alger Républicain* and *Soir-Républicain*, newspapers in Algiers. On these papers he was soon assigned duty as an investigative reporter. His reports brought factual and, therefore, critical attention to the inadequacies of the French administration of Algerian affairs.

In the city of Algiers itself official incompetence drew criticism and scorn from Camus in the columns of *Alger Républicain*. The paper assaulted the City Council: The non-attentive action of councilmen during the reading of the municipal budget was headlined as "The Municipal Fairy Tale." The mayor's conduct of his office was assailed. In one case, the mayor had suspended seven municipal employees for what Camus considered insufficient reasons. Attitudes and motives were ascribed to the official. The mayor's action was called odious and illegal, and the word "grotesque" frequently appeared. The mayor's action, said Camus, made him the hated adversary.

From Tiaret, a town well away from the city, a man named Michel Hodent appealed to *Alger Républicain* for assistance. Hodent, a government agency official in agricultural affairs, said he had been wrongly accused of thievery. In the consequent "Hodent Affair," Camus pressed for justice in this case of alleged malfeasance in office. The matter was pursued through twelve issues of *Alger Républicain*.

Before the man's trial, the paper printed an open letter to the Governor-General of Algeria: "There are no small injustices, nor small reparations. There is injustice and its thousand faces." By effecting the executive release of Hodent, Camus wrote, "You will have saved a man from the hate that he feels mounting in him. And in a world in which misery and absurdity make so many people lose the quality of being human, saving a single one amounts to saving oneself and with oneself a little of the human future that we all hope for." The Governor-General, by "giving his dignity back to a single man [could bring] a little more truth into a world where the lie and hatred would not always be able to triumph."

The government's case against Hodent evaporated when witnesses testified that they were genuine, and not the "fictitious customers" asserted in the prosecution's case. The prosecution's claims thus refuted, Hodent was released after four months in prison. But he was recalled on charges later shown to be equally false. Some other men, said to be accomplices, also were accused.

So many charges and reversals made the whole affair appear to be a monstrous joke. But Camus could not dismiss it so lightly. It was a joke only if he could keep from thinking "that this joke has cost four months in prison and the dishonoring of a generous man; much pain and suffering to a woman [Hodent's wife] who awaited her child; and the humiliation of some ten poor devils who suddenly sensed that their liberty was only in name and that their dignity had no other sense than that which a derisory justice was willing to give it."

The final article sympathized with the man's plight, even after his acquittal. "It is not inconsequential when people remove a man's illusions—that they destroy in a day what he has taken years to construct. Much time will be necessary to repair so much wrong."

While writing for *Alger Républicain* in the early summer of 1939, Camus conducted an extensive inquiry into the living conditions of the Kabyles, an indigenous people living in the mountainous area east of Algiers. There both the people and the land reminded him of Greece. But, while in Greece the marvel and glory of the human body are lifted up, "in no country that I know has the body appeared to me more humiliated than in the Kabylie. . . . The misery of this country is dreadful. . . . There is no spectacle more heartbreaking than this misery in the middle of one of the most beautiful countries of the world."

Again and again things seemed to Camus to be "out of joint" in the Kabylie. His articles were filled with facts and figures of population density; ratio of doctors to people; prices and wages; educational provision; and living conditions—all distinctly meager. Yet, "Never had the Kabylie seemed more beautiful to me than in the midst of this hasty and disordered springtime. . . . But I do not have the heart to evoke it here. I leave it to the imagination of each one to do that: to place the setting of these flower-covered mountains, of this sky without a wrinkle, of these magnificent evenings, around the ulcer-corroded face and the pus-filled eyes of a miserable Kabyle beggar."

Such wrenching contradictions were often apparent. On one occasion, in the hills above Tizi-Ouzou, he and a Kabyle friend watched the sunset. "And at that hour when the shadow descends the mountains onto that splendid land and brings relaxation to the heart of the most hardened man, I knew, however, that there was no peace for those on the other side of the valley who gathered around a griddle cake of bad barley."

He was so struck by the conditions that he feared his capacity to temper the emotions he felt. "I well know that [the reporting] must be restrained in order to give more force to the indignation we want to be felt. But I am not sure I am capable of that restraint. . . . I went to the Kabylie with the deliberate intention of telling what was good. But I've seen nothing. The misery filled my eyes at once. I saw it everywhere. It followed me everywhere."

The series concluded with articles on governmental action in the area. "[Here] I should like to give proof that I have not brought an exclusive taste for the description of a misery which appeared desperate to me. But [in] this harrowing story of an unprecedented situation, I hope . . . the numerous aspects of that misery may not dispel the pity which may have been awakened."

The level of health and medical services was so minimal that it was "distressing to record, even more so if one remembers that this people pursues its miserable existence in one of the healthiest regions of the world."

Provisions for education, on the other hand, were overdone. "The symbol of this absurd policy [stands in] the Aghrib region, one of the most unproductive of the Kabylie. . . . There, in the middle of this wilderness without a person to be seen, rose the sumptuous school of Aghrib as the very image of uselessness."

This series of articles, specific and detailed, challenged the imposition of French standards on non-European peoples. Naturally, the French authorities were disturbed by these descriptions and revelations of maladroit administration. Camus's obvious empathy with the victims of this mis-administration put him, once again, in conflict with the establishment.

Shortly after the Kabylie series, Camus was assigned to cover what became known as the "Grand Muphti Affair." The government had accused Cheik el Okbi and Abbas Turqui of murdering the Grand Muphti. But the case had not been prosecuted for three full years. Then the Cheik and his co-defendant were finally brought to trial. The paper's column headings announced the story: "History of a Crime. The Assassination of the Muphti. . . . In Three Years, Inspector Chennouf has not learned much about the assassination of the Muphti, but, on the other hand, he has forgotten a lot." Two days later the paper reported, "The Advocate General refuses to sustain the unbelievable accusation brought against Cheik el Okbi and Abbas Turqui." Conclusion of the case came quickly: "The Criminal Court, recognizing the innocence of Cheik el Okbi and of Abbas Turqui, has acquitted them."

Cheik el Okbi and Camus were to meet again, years later, when Camus traveled to Algeria to seek support for his "Appeal for a Civil Truce" in the French/Algerian War. Their friendship had lasted through the years.

In his biography of Camus, Herbert R. Lottman questions the acquittal which Camus's articles had supported. Lottman cites assertions and counter-assertions made about the el Okbi case some years later. With information drawn from his numerous contacts, Lottman describes with commendable thoroughness the complexity of the case. Camus, he claims, was on the wrong side in the case, drawn there by his liberalism. Lottman does concede, however, that the assembled testimony is not definitive. Olivier Todd goes even farther in his biography, asserting that "Camus let himself be exploited because of his contempt for the colonial administration."

Whether el Okbi was guilty or not, Camus at the time was responding in solidarity with an accused, with members of the

Arab community, with people oppressed by the very group to which Camus himself unquestionably belonged.

Camus clearly demonstrated deep affinity with the victims and the underclasses in Algeria. Yet, after his successes in mainland France, he was accused of being disingenuous in his later championing of the poor. Jean-Paul Sartre, for instance, in denying that Camus spoke for the poor and deprived any more than he, said, "You are an advocate who says, 'These are my brothers,' because that is the word with the most chance of making the jury cry." But those who suspected Camus's sincerity surely were unaware of his early activity in Algeria. Or, knowing of it, they refused to be affected by his disturbing accounts of victims and near-victims who were in the careless hands of rulers set over them.

Camus's investigative reporting showed his solidarity with victims. In a new assignment as a newspaper editor, he revealed his rebellious character.

After writing for *Alger Républicain*, in 1938 and '39, Camus became editor of *Soir Républicain*—the two papers were owned by the same people. With the beginning of World War II, censorship became a critical problem. It propelled Camus and the paper into head-on controversy with the authorities.

In a section called "Under the Lights of War," the paper reported news of the war, but also boldly marshalled controversial ideas about war in general—serious reflections on war and warring. Pre-war reprints and excerpts of political and literary works showed the underside of war, questioning its efficacy and its wisdom. Naturally, the authorities were aroused.

A series of articles dealt with World War I and the bases for peace at that time. "Truly, this text teaches nothing to anyone," insisted Camus. "The way the war of 1914 has been impressed in our flesh and in our living memory is more instructive than all the resumes in the world. Nevertheless [the article] has been censored. We must note that to give coherence to the rest of our study."

A following issue set forth a brief history of the formation of the League of Nations and gave the provisions of the Treaty of Versailles. Numerous deletions were made by the censors, and Camus noted that "we continue to utilize the Manual of History Malet-Isaac, currently used in [French] institutions of public education."

The censors were inept. Some inclusions were censored, while others, equally revealing, were not. "The possibility of a change of regime in France, passage from the parliamentarian form of government to a dictatorship pure and simple," stated by a member of the National Assembly, was allowed. But the censors cut Aldous Huxley's proposals for preventing war. "[Huxley] has been censored," said the editors, "as have been Victor Hugo and Voltaire. A little more patience and all French literature will be put under the index."

The paper happily quoted Edouard Daladier, the current French leader, when he said, at the Chamber of Deputies, "We French present ourselves before the eyes of the universe with our genius intact . . . our poets and our scholars attentive to the hopes and the miseries of all men. . . . No one dreams of separating France in war from that radiant France which has contributed to the awakening of all people."

"This is well-said," noted the paper. "And to show our accord we shall cite among the great men who have aided in making France radiant: Victor Hugo, Pascal, Voltaire"—all of whom had been censored in the column. "When we have found a text which is both intelligent and non-censorable . . . well-written and free of bureaucratese, we shall give it to our readers. That day we shall also have succeeded in squaring the circle."

Near the end of the paper's battle with the censors the death of the "anarchist" Jean Grave was reported. But the word "anarchist" was censored. Other papers, said *Soir*, were more modest, referring to the dead man only as a "writer and sociologist." But a few days later *Dépêche Algerienne* was allowed to use the expunged word. "We are happy to see today," said *Soir*, "that [censors] give us satisfaction, that they are willing to authorize the *Dépêche Algerienne* to print the frightful word 'anarchist' which, by inadvertence, they did not authorize us to write."

Finally, government authorities, repeatedly buffeted in the pages of the two newspapers, exercised the ultimate censorship. They ordered both papers to suspend operations. The papers' administrators, in appealing to the authorities for reconsideration, protested that Camus had been warned and reproved for his actions. The paper's owners blamed Camus (and, to a lesser extent, Pascal Pia, also a member of the staff) for the problems. But the authorities held their ground. Both *Soir Républicain* and *Alger Républicain* were disenfranchised. Camus himself became persona non grata, and had to take various kinds of work to support himself.

Camus's comportment as a journalist in Algeria is revealing. There is recognizable concord between his solidarity with victims and the rebellious practice of his journalism. His empathy, his solidarity with victims, was admirable, but dangerous, in the eyes of many of his fellow French Algerians. He was often imprudent in the directness of his criticisms of authority, and unwise in provoking that authority. He seems to have been reckless—or arrogant, as others were later to insist about him in other circumstances—in using his evident gifts of expression.

What can be said? Camus, a young man, may not have recognized the extent of the danger caused by sympathy for victims and public criticism of authorities. He may have been more naive than daring. But later events show his activities in

Algiers as the first of many similar ones, all consonant with the stance of rebellion which he was to enunciate thoroughly, years later, in *The Rebel*.

II

Contraries and Contradictions

Early on, as we have seen, Camus demonstrated his feelings of solidarity. But solitariness, its contrary, is equally discernible, as Camus depicted in the story of Daru in "The Guest." In his literary writings Camus's inclination and contentment in being solitary is discerned.

While in Algeria Camus began the literary course which brought him prominence in France and the world. *L'Envers et L'Endroit*, his first book, is a book of contraries; and the title announces this, one of several possible translations, *The Reverse and the Obverse*, being the most literal. This collection of his early writings differs from the militant articles and editorials in his newspaper work. Quiet and tempered pieces, some of them story-like, he later called them "essays" (in the French meaning of "attempts" or "trials"), since they did not measure up to his matured literary standards.

Years later, after both controversy and fame had troubled Camus, he looked back on these early writings and agreed to republish them. He said, "I myself know that my headwaters are in *L'Envers et L'Endroit*, in that world of poverty and light where I lived for a long time; and whose remembrance still preserves me from the two contrary dangers which threaten every artist: resentment and satisfaction."

The statement speaks for himself and to his detractors. He acknowledges and gratefully affirms the formative significance of his impoverished childhood. And he asserts that those lesser beginnings have also protected him from taking on the negative attitudes of those smug ones who resented his fame.

Drawn largely from life in Belcourt, his working class neighborhood in Algiers, the works exhibit the personal understanding and empathy characteristic of Camus. His feeling of solidarity is with the "lower class"—the less-fortunate, the impoverished, and the victims of society. But his firm appreciation of and his strong appetite for his own solitariness is also revealed. The ironic combination may account in part for his later willingness to stand alone, to go another way than that of associates—deportment often criticized in the midst of his lauded career.

The pieces came from Camus's youth and young manhood. They were collected and first published by Edmond Charlot, in Algiers, in 1937, when Camus was 23 years old. Thus they were written by him at the hinge of twenty, some, probably, during his teen years. Yet, remarkably, the focus of many of them is on old people. Many of these people, furthermore, are at the edge of the end of life.

His attention to the frail old ones may have been due in part to his own experience of the vulnerability of serious illness. When he was seventeen an attack of tuberculosis brought death close. The suddenness of the attack, assailing him in the middle of a strong and athletic teenhood, must have heightened his perception of the dark, joyless side of life.

That perception was not without precedent. His mother, suffering heavy blows of misfortune, lived a difficult life, yet silently accepted it. World War I deprived her of her husband. The shock of his loss, apparently, brought on a speech impediment, with consequent near-muteness. Widowed, with two young children, and minimal means for supporting them, her household was one of poverty. The dark side of life touched her, even in this land of sun and light. Her son had to have felt the somber, even stoic, endurance of the mother for whom he repeatedly expressed his strong love.

The title of the collection is revealing in itself. Life has its back and its front side, its outside and its inside, its wrong side and its right side. Since a garment is expected to be worn right side out, the order in the title is notable: *The Wrong Side and the Right Side*. Yes, the one side may be preferred, but both are reality. The reverse side of the coin is as much the coin as is the obverse.

The book includes three character sketches, one of them featuring his grandmother. In the first of the three, he tells of an old woman in another family. She is provided little more than her material needs. She is granted only a corner of the house, and pleads for whatever she gets, though she would prefer death to being in someone's charge.

Camus wrote, "Her voice had become querulous . . . the voice of the market." The narrator, a young man there on a visit to the family, thought that being in someone's care was better than dying. "But that only proved one thing: that, clearly, he had never been in charge of someone." He noticed the old woman's rosary and her devotion, but heard the woman's daughter say, "'Here's someone who still prays!' The sick one replied, 'What's it do to you?'" and heard, "'Nothing but get on my nerves.' So the old woman shut up, fixing a long, reproachful gaze on her daughter." The young man, "with an immense, unfocused pain cramping his chest," heard the old woman's plaint, "'She will see, when she's old. She'll need someone, too!'"

To the young man the old woman appeared to be neglected, barely short of abandonment, "freed of everything except

God. . . . But hope in God and a reborn life is of no force against the interests of humans."

He was invited to dinner, which the old woman did not eat. Then he was asked to continue his visit by going with his hosts to a movie, the old woman not invited. As the family moved out, "they went to her to hug her and wish her a good evening. . . . Only the young man remained. . . . She did not want to be alone. . . . She was afraid . . . [so], attaching herself to the only one who had shown interest in her, she wouldn't release his hand. . . . The young man was ill at ease.

"He felt himself placed before the most dreadful misfortune he'd ever known: that of a sick old woman they'd abandoned to go to a movie. . . . For a second, he felt a fierce hatred for that old woman and thought of slapping her around."

Finally breaking away, leaving the woman to her dark and despairing thoughts, he joined the others, "already in the street. An obstinate remorse troubled the young man. He lifted his eyes to the lighted window, a great dead eye in the silent house. The eye closed. The daughter of the sick old woman said to the young man, 'She always turns out the light when she's alone. She likes to stay in the dark.'"

No doubt "the young man" was the young Camus, his sensitivity heightened by his own experience of the sudden onslaught of serious illness in his teen years.

His empathy with this old woman is remarkable—more so when compared with his depiction of his grandmother. This old woman wins almost unqualified sympathy and concern—but his grandmother engendered no pity in Camus, as the sketch about her reveals.

His grandmother ran the household of five during Camus's boyhood. Camus and his older brother, their mother and her brother, and the boys' grandmother made up the family. Camus's mother was usually silent, speaking only with difficulty; and his uncle, too, was almost mute. His mother was not well, but worked outside the home as a domestic to support the family. Lucien, Camus's brother, some four years older, worked when old enough, and brought in some money. His mother's work left the children's upbringing to her mother, who ruled them with a stick, sometimes evoking their mother's plea for restraint. The grandmother dominated everyone.

Camus recalled a return visit, when a young man. He wrote of Algiers, the city, and the Arab quarter within it, the softness of the evenings, his mounting of the stairs "by heart," the domestic dynamics he remembered—and of his grandmother.

"Above her bed you could see a picture of her: less than five years old . . . immense, clear, cold eyes; the carriage of a queen which she gave up only in old age and sometimes tried to recover in the streets."

In her mature years those eyes could make her grandson blush. They often fixed him as a boy, when visitors were present, as she demanded, "'Who do you prefer, your mother or your grandmother?' The game intensified when his mother herself was present. For, every time, the child responded: 'My grandmother,' with a great burst of love for his mother who was always silent. When visitors were astonished by that preference, his mother said: 'She raised him.'"

The older woman had her good points, but the two boys saw her as a comic actor, filling the role of manager, yet overplaying her importance and her troubles. She could be noisily sick and, when begged to go to bed, remind them of the cooking she had to do and her task of running the house. "'I do everything here.' And again: 'What would become of you if I disappeared!'"

The boys learned to ignore both her complaints and her illnesses. When the doctor was called in for a serious malady, "The younger of the two children persisted in seeing only a new comedy in all this, a more polished deception. He was not disturbed. The woman had oppressed him too much to make these first thoughts pessimistic. And there was a kind of desperate courage in lucidity and the refusal to love."

Though her grandson thought she was playing one of her games, this time she was indeed ill, seriously ill. He, "it now seemed, had understood nothing. He could not divest himself of the idea that the last and most monstrous simulations of that woman had just been played before him." But he kept his emotions secret, crying only on the day she was buried, even then with fear of being insincere.

At the cemetery, the occasion did not prevent awareness of his surroundings. "It was a beautiful winter day, spread with sunbeams. In the blue of the sky, spangled with yellow, you could discern the cold. From the cemetery, dominating the city, you could see the beautiful transparent sun falling on the bay, trembling with light, like a moist lip." For Camus the dark grave and burial did not obscure, may even have heightened, the province of beauty and light.

The third of these three character sketches told of an old man socializing with some young men. He was holding forth about his youth. He was enjoying himself. But the young men listening soon tired of the stories, even though the old man embellished his telling with lies and exaggerations. They walked away, and the old man realized he was no longer amusing, just old. He was left alone, despite his efforts to hold his audience. The young Camus observed: "No longer being heard: that is what is terrible when one's old; one's condemned to silence and solitude—telling him that he is soon going to die. And an old man who is going to die is useless, even disturbing and treacherous."

Reflectively, Camus observes that "men build against their coming old age. . . . They want to be the foreman, in order to retire to a small villa. But once arrived at old age, they know very well that that is wrong. They have need of other people for protection."

As for the old man himself, left standing alone, "the streets were now darker and less peopled." Eyes closed, facing "life which carried the rumblings of the city and the silly, indifferent smile of the heavens, he was alone, stripped, naked, already dead."

But the man's wife, Camus imagines, is unaware of his distress. "Is it necessary to describe the other side of the coin? One suspects that in a dirty and dark room the old wife sets the table—with dinner ready, she sits down, looks at the clock, waits a while, and then begins to eat with appetite. She thinks, 'He's in one of his moods.' That says it all."

The stories of these old people raised questions for Camus. "Does not all this fit together? The utter truth: A woman abandoned to take in a movie; an old man no longer listened to; a death which redeems nothing; and then, on the other hand, all the light of the world."

The questions and the disparity between hard life and the world's beneficence brought resolution as well: "What does it matter, if you accept everything? Here are three similar, yet different destinies. Death for everyone, but each his own death. After all, the sun warms even our bones."

Experience of the dark and the light, of depreciation and appreciation, of the wrong and the right sides, of the inside and the outside marked Camus's individual life as well. Details can be found in Herbert R. Lottman's *Albert Camus: A Biography*, or Olivier Todd's *Albert Camus, A Life*, but will be briefly noted here.

His illness affected him in his youth and throughout his life, adversely impacting his academic potential—since the French system denied the *aggregation* to those with significant health problems—and forcing recesses, now and again, during his several careers. His first marriage, in 1934, when he was about twenty-one years old, was a mistake which soon resulted in separation and eventual divorce.

In the latter sections of *L'Envers et L'Endroit* Camus is solitary. Whether in foreign places or forced isolation because of his tuberculosis, he is essentially alone. Though people appear in the pieces, they are not in direct relation with the author, but are observed only. But he relates to the settings, on the other hand, with intensity, deeply affected by features of his immediate environment.

Strong awareness of life's contraries is evidenced in the writings which issued from a trip in 1936, when Camus, his wife, and a male friend toured parts of Europe. Camus found Eastern Europe not at all to his taste; it did not match the ambiance of his homeland. In the latter part of their journeying, Camus stayed alone for a week in Prague.

Ignorant of the language, alone in the crowds on the streets—everything contributed to his low and lowered spirits. The dullness of the city, the flatness of the land, smells of sourness, poor tasting food, his lack of money, the remoteness of the people, and his virtual muteness reinforced a natural despair and feeling of absurdity.

Prague exercised the attraction of incompatibility for him, reinforcing the lowness of his spirit. In *La Mort dans L'Ame* (*Death in the Soul*) Camus reveals the depressing atmosphere which he would evoke again in the darkest of his later writings, *The Misunderstanding*, a play set in Czechoslovakia.

In his hotel room, one day, several rappings on the door of the next room aroused his curiosity. When, after a time, leaving his room for lunch, he sees one of the hotel staff approach the next room door, try it, and rap several times, Camus goes on out, without asking about the matter. "But," he wrote, "in the streets of Prague, I was followed by a sad foreboding. . . . I lunched, at last, but with increasing distaste."

On returning to the hotel, he wrote, "I climbed the stairs rapidly, and quickly found myself facing what I expected . . . the dull light . . . projected . . . the shadow of a dead man laid out on the bed and that of a policeman standing guard by the body. . . . That light upset me. It was authentic, a true light of life, of the afternoon of life, a light which makes one aware that he is living."

Though sure that the man was not a suicide, Camus nevertheless was deeply touched by the event, his feeling of solidarity once more manifest. "I entered my room precipitately and threw myself on my bed. A man like many others, short and stout, if I believed the shadow. He'd been dead a long time, no doubt. And life continued in the hotel. . . . He had arrived there, suspecting nothing, and he died alone."

When he left Prague, Camus moved away from days on the dark side, where circumstances reinforced his native despair and his sensitivity to the absurdities of life. On the train, en route to Italy, he was expectant: "I was like a convalescent nourished on bouillon and thinking of the first piece of bread that he will eat. A light was born. I know now: I was ready for happiness."

Stopping in Vicenza, Italy, Camus rediscovered color, light, the warm sun, smiling people, pleasant smells, sloping hills, long vistas. He was at home again, under the sun of the Mediterranean. "I walk along the road . . . with slow steps, oppressed by so much ardent beauty. . . . And, in the last light, on the facade of a villa, I read: '*In magnificentia naturae, resurgit spiritus.*'"

Under the prominent sun of Vicenza, Camus realized its significance for him. "I have not yet spoken of the sun. Just as I took a long time to comprehend my attachment and my love for the world of poverty where I passed my childhood, it's only now that I glimpse the lesson of the sun and the lands which gave me birth."

Yet memory of the "horizontal shadow of the little, short, stout man" persisted against the beauty of the present place—a juxtaposing reminiscent of his newspaper articles reporting the disparity between the jarring plight of the Kabyles and the soft beauty surrounding them.

"This country led me into the heart of myself, facing my secret anguish. But it was the anguish of Prague and it was not. How to explain? Certainly, within this Italian plain, peopled with trees, sun, and smiles, I have caught, more than elsewhere, the odor of death and of inhumanity which pursued me for a month."

In the glorious beauty of northern Italy he most fully felt the distress of his time in Prague. The vibrant life of Vicenza did not overcome the remembered smells of decay.

All seemed to rouse a deep sense of a classic Greek version of immortality. "For me, [there is] no promise of immortality in this land. What could revive me in my spirit, without eyes to see Vicenza, without hands to touch the grapes of Vicenza, without skin to feel the caress of the night on the road from Monte Berico to the villa Valmarana?"

But, if immortality was not for Camus, he nevertheless felt a large need. "I had need of grandeur. I found it in the confrontation of my profound despair and the secret indifference of one of the most beautiful landscapes in the world. In that I found the strength to be courageous and conscious at the same time."

Contraries evoke one another—disjunction is in Camus's nature of things. Awareness confronts indifference. The light evokes the dark. Life deeply felt throws the spirit back to past unease and death. Thus Camus set forth his early experience of absurdity, through which he was passing, and foreshadowed the idea of lucidity he was to develop in his later writings

"I return often to Prague and to the mortal days I lived there. I have found my city. Sometimes, no more than a sharp odor of cucumber and vinegar arouses my anxiety. Then I must think of Vicenza. But both are dear to me and I hardly separate my love of light and life from my secret attachment to the desperate experience I've wanted to describe."

Camus closes this essay with a short parable. "In the suburb of Algiers there's a little cemetery with gates of black iron. If you go to the far end, you discover a valley, with the bay at its depth. You can dream a long time over this offering which smiles with the sea. But when you retrace your steps, you find a plaque, "Eternal Regrets," on an abandoned tomb. Happily, there are idealists to arrange things."

In the last parts of *L'Envers et L'Endroit*, "Amour de Vivre" ("Love of Living") continues the linking of the downside and the upside, though the title might suggest otherwise. Solitariness is enjoyed, even in the presence of other people. In Palma, Majorca, Camus described a tavern full of men devoted to noise and drinking.

"A sudden cymbal clash and a woman jumped brusquely into the tiny circle in the middle of the cabaret . . . [a woman with] a young girl's face, sculpted in a mountain of flesh." Camus was astounded at her size. His description reveals his wonder about the young woman's attraction for the men. "Hands on her hips, dressed in a yellow net, the meshes making a chess-board of swollen white flesh, she smiled, and each corner of her mouth sent a series of little waves of flesh to her ears. In the room, there was excitement without limit. One sensed that this girl was known, loved, awaited."

The woman fascinated her audience, drawing them along through every turn of her act, though neither her features nor her performance seemed to explain the enchantment she extorted. But they were with her, without question, joining her in singing. "At the refrain, the girl, turning round and round, holding her breasts in her hands, opening her red, moistened mouth, repeated the melody in unison with the audience, until everybody was standing in the uproar."

In his description Camus linked tawdry vibrancy and lively despair. "Fixed in the center, sticky with sweat, uncombed, she raised up her massive figure, swollen in her yellow netting. Like a defiled goddess coming out of the water—her face stupid and base, her eyes hollow, she was alive only through a tiny quivering of her knees—the ignoble and exalting symbol of life, with the despair of her empty eyes, and the thick sweat of her belly . . . [sic]."

Was she the symbol of life for the men, who saw what Camus saw, who participated more than he? We do not know, though they seem to have experienced something more than beer and titillation. But surely for Camus the girl was symbol: the occasion, judged by its effect on the men, was ritual and ceremony.

After the tumultuous tavern scene Camus experienced a contrasting scene in the San Francisco quarter of Palma. There, Camus found all quiet and languid. There were scenes of beauty in the shadows of old buildings, flights of pigeons, "odors of silence," people here and there. "A woman was drawing water from the well. In an hour, a minute, a second, right now, perhaps, everything could crumble. And yet the miracle was continuing. The world endured, modest, ironic, and discreet (like certain gentle and prudent kinds of the friendship of women). A balance prevailed, colored, however, by all the apprehension of its own end."

Though apprehension persisted, the balance was still maintained, the world continued. Camus's awareness of potentials—of the wrong side in face of the right side, of the right side opposed to the wrong side . . . of the other side, in short—accompanied him wherever he was, and in whatever state he found himself.

"All my love of living was there: a silent passion for what might be escaping me, a bitterness under a flame. . . . I marvel that one can find certitudes and rules for life here in the lands along the Mediterranean, that here one's reason is satisfied and one's optimism and social sense are warranted. For finally, then, it struck me: a world not made to the measure of man— but one which enveloped man . . . not gratitude . . . but only Nothingness could be born in me when facing these sun-crushed landscapes. There is no love of living without despair of living."

His visit continued on Ibiza, the smallest of the Balearics. Responding to life observed there and on Majorca, he said, "I wanted to love as one wants to cry. I felt that each hour of sleep from now on would be stolen from life . . . [sic] that is, from times of object-less desire. As in those vibrant hours in the cabaret in Palma and the cloister of San Francisco, I was motionless and tense, powerless against the immense impulse of wanting to take the whole world in my hands."

Here and elsewhere, Camus discloses his marked capacity to discover revelation in unexpected places, often found in contraries.

The final section of *L'Envers et L'Endroit* bears the title of the collection itself. It sums up the whole, then, and with characteristic linkages. But, whereas the early parts of the book were relational, in these as in the travel sections immediately preceding, Camus is solitary, observing others, but speaking of himself.

In these last pages, Camus tells of an old woman who, with a small inheritance, purchased an existing, vacant, elegant tomb for herself, at a modest cost. She had her name engraved on it in gold capitals. She offered prayers in it, veritably loved it, visited it every Sunday afternoon, her sole recreation. "By a singular symbol, she even understood one day that she was dead in the eyes of the world. On All Saints' day, arriving later than usual, she found the doorstep piously strewn with violets. Compassionate, thoughtfully attentive strangers, facing this tomb left without flowers, shared some of theirs, and honored the memory of this dead woman abandoned by herself."

A contrary case follows immediately, with no more than a paragraph break to mark the change. The scene is now in a room with extremely limited visual connection with the world, and the occupant is not there by choice. It is a forced confinement, no other humans present. Through the single window: rays of sunlight, shadows of branches, smells of the grass; and the colors of a bouquet in the room. "It is enough: a solitary emerging gleam and I'm filled with a confused and bewildering joy. It is a January afternoon which thus sets me facing the inverse of the world.

"Who am I and what can I do, except enter into the play of foliage and the light? . . . And if I try to comprehend and to relish this delicate savor which reveals the secret of the world, it is myself which I find in the depth of the universe. Myself—that is, this extreme emotion which delivers me from the setting."

Camus then contrasts these two responses to life-in-the-face-of-death: A woman who confines herself for devotion in the expectant contemplation of death; a man (himself) who, though confined by serious illness, discovers the secret of life in the threat of death. As in his travel experiences, unpleasant, even desperate conditions excite a strong impulse of life-affirmation.

L'Envers et L'Endroit draws to conclusion with attention to the end of life. "Just now, other things, people, and the tombs they buy. But let me set apart this minute in the fabric of time. . . . Today is a stopping place, and my heart is moving to the encounter with myself. If anguish still grips me, it is in feeling this impalpable instant slip between my fingers like drops of mercury. . . . Let those who want to, turn their backs on the world. I do not pity myself since I regard myself to be awakened. In this hour, all my kingdom is in this world."

In the context of his confinement, "this world" is that coming into his presence through the window of his room— natural surroundings, without people. Others may turn their backs on this world; Camus is awakened in it.

Yet, though his encounter here is in a peopleless world, Camus is not altogether oblivious of others. "This sun and these shadows; this warmth and the cold which comes from the depth of the air: I ask myself about things dying and men suffering— since everything is written in this window where the sky pours out its plenty in the encounter with my pity."

Pity for "things dying . . . and men suffering," had not been evinced, however, for the woman who had turned away from the world in preference for her carefully tended tomb. And other people are only momentarily in focus, for he is in isolation. Here the world comes to him only in fragments. But it is enough. He relates to the partial world presented in his room. The essential for that relating, however, is not entirely clear. He presents and withdraws, and again proposes what seems to be required: "What counts is to be human, very simply. No, what counts is to be true and then everything is inscribed: humanity and simplicity."

Camus speaks of the sensate world, and of himself related to it. He is with, in, of the world—a world of phenomena, a permeable and enterable world. "When am I more true than when I am the world? I am filled before having desired. Eternity is here and I hoped for it."

Then, in reiteration of his simple acceptance of the world as it is, with its wrong side and its right side, Camus puts happiness aside, in favor of awareness: "Now, being happy is no longer what I want, but only to be conscious."—to fit into the world enveloping him, without expenditure of effort to explain that world.

The book concludes with contraries. "One man contemplates and another hollows out his tomb: how distinguish them? Men and their absurdity?" he asks, though the reader surely knows which stance Camus prefers. Then he notes the world around him, "Here is the smile of the sky, the light expands, and it is soon summer, no?" And he acknowledges other people, "Here are the eyes and the voices of those one must love."

But his responses to the world and to men are different. "I hold on to the world by all my actions, to men by all my pity and my appreciation." Yes, other people are involved—"those one must love" curiously implies a duty to love—but at a remove, whereas the world is embraced by all his actions. "Pity" and "appreciation" are extended to people, but the world draws him in. Camus appears to be more at-one with the world than with people.

"Between this one side and the other side of the world I do not want to choose, I do not like it that one may choose." One side and the other: the dark side and the bright side or, perhaps, the inside and the outside—Camus's singular, internal life and his relational, external life.

The book's conclusion lifts two words—"lucid" and "ironic." The one foreshadows the trait of lucidity, which will be developed in *The Myth of Sisyphus*. The other will receive less direct attention, though Camus would later say that irony was a largely overlooked feature of his work. Attitudes related to the two terms are not popular, he said. "People do not want you to be lucid and ironic," perhaps because that challenges personal philosophies or beliefs.

But he saw virtue in both postures, appealing, ironically, for as much attention to "the light" as to death. "There's great courage in keeping your eyes as open to the light as to death."

The down side is again stressed when he wonders "how to speak of the tie which leads from this devouring love of life to this secret despair. If I listen to irony, taking cover in the depth of things, it reveals itself slowly. Blinking its little, clear eye it says: 'Live as if . . .' [sic]. Despite much research, that is the totality of my knowledge."

And he appeals to irony with his final, and telling, sally against that stance which lets death dictate to life. "After all, I am not sure I am right. But that is not important if I think of that woman whose story I was told. She was dying and her daughter dressed her for burial while she was alive. It seems that it's easier when the limbs are not stiff. It is curious, all the same, how we live among hurrying people."

In these early writings, Camus reveals personal benefits he gained in trying circumstances. From the contraries of dark side-light side, wrong side and right side, inside and outside, came insight and even jubilation. Implicitly, he recognized that these gains are not acquired automatically. They arise from the practice of awareness—of seeing both faces of the stuff of the world.

These essays contrast with Camus's early journalistic writings—both in substance and in tone. The essays recount personal experiences or record his responses to the observed behavior of other people. They are quiet, reflective, and assenting.

On the other hand, the newspaper reports deal with the events and struggles of daily public life. The reporting is aggressive, contentious, and advocative.

Camus's illness and the plight of the Kabyles exemplify the differences. Camus's calm acceptance of chronic tuberculosis apparently came from his awareness of the wrong and the right sides in life. He endured confinement. He did not complain about his illness, even to the point of valuing the solitariness it caused. He did not perceive himself as a victim.

But he had not accepted the distress of the Kabyles calmly (or that of others of whom he wrote). The dissonance between the beauty of the Kabylie and the people's plight there struck Camus forcefully. Their debilitating circumstances won his sympathy. He felt solidarity with them, and saw them to be victims.

In the face of his own trying circumstances he appeared to be without need of solidarity. He was sufficient unto himself, uncomplaining about his situation. But, out of concern for the distress of the Kabyles, he stood in solidarity with them.

Awareness and acceptance appear to be the two touchstones for understanding the differing responses. Clearly, the plight of the Kabyles was imposed upon them. It need not have been—and that was simply unacceptable, articulately so for Camus, mutely so for the Kabyles. His own illness, on the other hand, was within the normal range of human experience, a product of the givens of the world, and he accepted it.

In his own life Camus successfully navigated through the absurd. But he showed that the absurdities of the Kabylie tragically afflicted the lives and the spirits of the Kabyles. (His later fictional works would present similar negatives effects of the absurd in the personages he created.)

What accounts for Camus's differing responses? The answer can only be conjecture. But, judging by Camus's later works, the source of the distressing circumstances accounts for his acceptance or rejection of them. The universal scheme of things was the cause of Camus's own strickenness. But the Algerian government was the source of the deprivations imposed on the Kabyles.

Circumstances arising from the primal givens of human life are simply to be accepted when responsive to no human amelioration. But when government intervention infringes peoples' lives the government is to be questioned, challenged, and even opposed.

Camus would thoroughly address the question of oppressive governments in *The Rebel*.

III

Absurd Beginnings

Camus's early works utilized rebellious thought. The observing and experiencing of contradictions and contraries brought perspective and insight. The absurd surfaced into recognition.

The subject of the absurd was addressed with three of Camus's works, deliberately connected. In *The Stranger*, *The Myth of Sisyphus*, and *Caligula* he examined the concept in a novel, a philosophical essay, and a play. The three were underway together, and which was first is not establishable, nor is it critical.

Meursault, lead character in *The Stranger*, in most of his acts, and for most of his life, is an unconscious rebel. His response to life is largely passive; he is oblivious or heedless of social convention. He unconsciously ignores convention, blithely and without reflection. The reader doesn't know what has brought Meursault to this stance, and Meursault doesn't know either. Camus's fictional character is an instinctive rebel.

With "'Your mother died today'" the story begins. But his mother's death is little more than the other things which make his life an endless succession of Monday, Tuesday, Wednesday . . . Meursault finds pleasure in neither accomplishment nor expectation. He simply accepts whatever the moment brings.

He imbibes that moment, whatever its quality. It is experienced with a shrug, not assessed, nor appraised, nor evaluated, but simply lived. Social convention has no standing against spontaneous, instant response to the moment.

On learning of his mother's death, Meursault regrets only the inconvenience for him. He travels to the rest home where she had lived. But other than that he does little or nothing to meet the expectations of those who knew his mother, who thought he would mourn. After the funeral he coolly returns to attend a funny movie and to enjoy a sexual liaison the day after his mother's funeral. Aware, vaguely, that he's not doing what's expected, he nevertheless continues living the moment as it comes to him—with Fernandel in a movie, with Marie Cardona at the beach and then in bed.

The reader grants Meursault some sympathy—elicited by his honesty in not feigning a remorse or sorrow he does not feel. The minor characters in this first section reinforce this empathy, for they are subtly caricatured versions of ordinary people. Their exaggerated expectations of a sorrowing son are unfulfilled, and they take Meursault to be a strange one. These excessive requirements elicit empathy for Meursault from readers who recognize that they too sometimes feel constrained to exhibit feelings which are not internally true.

The readers' sympathy is further heightened by Meursault's ambiguously admirable acts in fraternizing with old Salamano and his mangy dog, and with Raymond Sintes, despite his unsavory reputation. Meursault, no doubt, knows that neither of these men can do anything for him. Yet he befriends them and does them favors, free, it seems, of self-serving.

Thus prepared, the reader accepts the next pieces of the pattern. Meursault casually accepts a shady proposition of Raymond's. He writes a letter to provoke Raymond's girl friend, and perjures himself to a policeman after the brawl with the girl.

The impulse of the moment; the instinct to help a friend; the belief—subconscious or not well-formed—that it really doesn't matter what he does: these all converge to prompt easy acquiescence and participation in a dirty deal. An act of moral naiveté, at best, his action is mindless deviation from any kind of ethics—it is thoughtless, amoral rebellion.

The pattern set, the series of events on the beach leads up to what Meursault calls the "fateful rap on the door of my undoing." Having cautioned Raymond against unconsidered action, having nonchalantly participated in Raymond's fight with the Arab—which leaves Raymond wounded and bleeding—Meursault, looking no farther ahead than the next moment, moves in a series of missteps toward the ending of any moral innocence he may have had.

Against good sense, Meursault returns to the beach from the cabin, carrying Raymond's revolver in his pocket. He turns the wrong way on the beach, he heads unreflectively toward the place where the Arab assailants had disappeared. At any moment he could have reversed the direction of his going. At no moment did he do so. Thus he put himself under the assaultive rays of the sun, thus he walked toward the knife-armed Arab, thus he responded to the flash of reflected heat from the knife, thus he let his finger press the finger, thus he stepped forward to fire four more rounds into the motionless body on the sands.

With those lethal shots begins the process of Meursault's becoming consciously absurd.

In the first part of *The Stranger*, Meursault is not unlike the young Camus revealed in *L'Envers et L'Endroit*. There is the same wide openness to elements of the world which graze against his person; the unusual level of awareness of items in his surroundings; the same pleasure in the inconsequential; the same third-person detachment in events in which he is first-person; the same acceptance of the underside of things.

But there is no semblance of the trait of solidarity with victims which motivated Camus, particularly in his newspaper work.

Events and circumstances in the second part of *The Stranger*, however, differ from those in the first. In the first Meursault is passive—except for the shooting. Passivity is possible because he is not subject to attack or assault. But in the second part his action on the beach inaugurates a new requirement. He must defend his strangeness. He rebels in retrospect.

The first part of *The Stranger* shows Meursault living passively, sensually, thoughtlessly, failing to meet expectations, stumbling into murder without a reason.

The second part portrays Meursault awakening, realizing that he is a stranger to general society, that he is on display as an oddity: a man who did not weep when his mother died. Yet, even when he recognizes that he's being tried for failing to conform, rather than for the murder he's committed, he scarcely enters into his legal defense. In failing to participate vigorously in that defense, he once again reveals his strangeness.

But, when the chaplain sounds the chord of "meaning," Meursault livens up strenuously. He becomes a conscious, aggressive rebel. The enjoyment of insignificant moments is replaced by the passion of assertion, a rising volume of protest aroused by the chaplain's talking about God. The energy, the flow of words, the clutching hands, the vehemence of utterance reveal a vivified rebel bursting out of passivity into actuation. Then, in full awareness of his revolt, he wishes that, at his execution, he may hear howls of execration from the people. He thus proclaims his difference from the others, he affirms his strangeness, he takes the role of the rebel. The release brought on by conscious rebellion brings fresh winds into his life, and he recognizes the benign indifference of the universe.

Meursault has been at home with the givens of the earth—the sea, the sounds, the flowing light of Algeria—by noting and accepting their impact on his senses. He relates to people in the same way. They are inputs in his sensuous life. He experiences shared moments, with no further linkage.

Though insignificant for him, however, those moments have significance for the others. Raymond Sintes sees Meursault as a pal. Marie Cardona wants to marry him. But he never felt close to those who felt close to him. For him, personal moments were no more than the other things of life—all to be felt, enjoyed, received, but elevated into nothing more. He was amiably indifferent to people—and observers perceived that as strangeness. He was a solitary stranger.

Meursault is an unconscious exponent of solipsism. Others are there, but they are of such little significance that they are not appraised for quality. Persons, along with other phenomena, are simply the elemental stuff which provides experience. The amount and extent of this experience constitute the only desirable things in life.

He had an extraordinary capacity to enjoy what was before him, and in that respect might well be emulated, for many people undervalue the little joys and pleasures close at hand. But he was oblivious or disdainful of others as persons and of the effect of his acts upon them. Any act was like another, for "it all comes to the same thing." What mattered was for the flow to continue. It was the quantity, and not the quality, of acts which was of importance.

Until nearly the end of the reader's acquaintance, Meursault focuses on quantity. He is a rebel of singular passivity, feeling the absurd, but not consciously aware of it.

But in the companion work, *The Myth of Sisyphus*, Sisyphus is fully conscious of the absurd. He is defiant of the gods and the scheme of things. He is a metaphysical rebel of high metabolism, energetically taking his rebellion to the very edge of the gods' domain.

Both men are alike in the constancy with which they maintain antagonism to the expected, to the accepted, to the ordered scheme of things. But they're unlike in that one disdains only the social scheme while the other actively defies the metaphysical order.

According to Camus, human beings are equipped with a yearning for order, for clarity, for unity, for meaning in this world. In *The Myth* Camus calls that yearning "nostalgia"—a primal feeling, inherent and basic, which is present in all humans. Nostalgia is authentic and necessary—and therefore must never be ignored. But it may win such allegiance as to become dangerous for one's humanity.

The strength of nostalgia accounts for the actions of the society surrounding Meursault—the officers and inmates of the old folks' home in Marengo, the little robot lady in Celeste's cafe, the magistrate interrogating Meursault, the defense attorney, those who attend the trial, the chaplain in Meursault's cell. Meursault is surrounded by people who have surrendered to nostalgia. He is in passive rebellion against this imperialism of the nostalgic. But his passivity is later transformed into ardor and revolt when the articulate representative of the nostalgic, the chaplain, accosts Meursault in his cell. In the fury of his response Meursault rejects those nostalgic constructions of humans which impose an order, a clarity, a meaning on a universe which has none. At the same time, most importantly, Meursault accepts the benign indifference of that universe.

Sisyphus, instead, feels the malevolent force of the universal scheme of things. That state of affairs condemns him. He is enraged against the gods who manage universal affairs. He scorns that which commits him to pushing rocks. He feels the dissonance between his sentence of condemnation and the sensuous satisfactions provided by the place in which he pushes. The way things are—condemnation, punishment, death—is unsatisfactory, irrational, non-acceptable. Sisyphus is at metaphysical odds with the order of the world. Condemned by the gods, he condemns their condemnation. He is a metaphysical rebel. He sees and acts against the irrational.

The absurd equation is composed of nostalgia and the irrational. Nostalgia seeks clarity but the irrational allows none. The universe is irrational. It is beyond the comprehension of humans, unfathomable, opaque. The universe is, and humans are in it. Though parts of it are explainable, it is basically obscure to humans. People live in the universe, are sustained within it, yet suffer unaccountably, condemned to death from their beginnings. Though not hostile to humans, the universe is benignly unkind. Such is the mixture of support and assault, of joy and suffering, of pleasure and pain, that the universe is incomprehensible. It is irrational.

Nostalgia and the irrational are the two elements of the absurd equation. They exist, they have their being, only in the presence of humans. They would not be without humankind. Nor, Camus implies, is a human fully human without some intimation of the two, and of oneself in their presence. Nostalgia, the irrational, and humans constitute the absurd.

It is possible to perceive the irrationality of the universe and respond with a shrug. Many people do—Meursault among them. But Camus asserts that this response is at the cost of suppressing what is native to humans: nostalgia. Loss or suppression of nostalgia is tacit acceptance of the irrationality of the universe, with no effort to seek the reason behind or within it. Yet that seeking is an authentic part of being fully human.

Camus has relatively little to say about those who give up on nostalgia and give in to the irrational. But he has much to say about the opposite trait—such high concern for nostalgia that the irrational is explained away. People too easily accept "explanations" of the meaning of the universe; or they create their own, believing that they have found the meaning; or they assume that, despite the evidence, there is a hidden meaning which would explain all if only it were known. They assert that they have discovered rational antidotes to the irrational. But they are mistaken. The irrational persists. To deny the irrational by retreat into the bastion of nostalgia is to commit a crime. Concession to nostalgia is of such immensity in import that Camus calls it philosophical suicide.

The absurd in *The Myth* is set forth in the language of advocacy, causing many readers to take it as an out-and-out espousal of the absurd as a philosophy of life. But the Preface gives a mild warning against such a reading. "The absurd . . . is considered in this essay as a starting point. . . . There will be found here merely the description, in the pure state, of an intellectual malady. No metaphysic, no belief is involved in it for the moment."

Further evidence that Camus was moving away from the absurd is found in the fact that *The Stranger* and *Caligula* were being written at the same time as *The Myth*. And these two cast serious doubt on the absurd. Camus addresses the "intellectual malady of the absurd" through a novel and a play as well as in the essay of *The Myth*.

The Myth of Sisyphus delineates the absurd, that divorce in the being of humans, who want to know, yet cannot fully know. Domiciled in a universe whose meaning is obscure—and equipped with thought, the composite of feelings and reason—humans experience a yearning to know while understanding that knowing is impossible. Though the universe is dense, humans have eyes that try to see into that density.

The feeling of the absurd is easily acquired, coming unbidden in the succession of days which lead inevitably to death and the cessation of days. Weariness of the flesh comes not from the flesh, but from the awareness of self as more than a rock which does not need to know. The weariness mounts until humans envy stones and covet the contentedness of hills and the stability of the measured rise and fall of the seas. Feeling, which brings zest and verve to life, brings also a sense of unease about the absurd necessity of dying.

The feeling of the absurd may be little more than restlessness and unease of spirit, a vague discontent with what life yields. The feeling may come from nothing more than unfocused boredom with a life in which not enough happens, though much may happen. The feeling can accompany a life of pleasantness, a pleasantness which, for no real reason, fails to bring happiness. Life, which seems to offer all, which may indeed give much, appears to be absurd and unfulfilling.

Probably everyone feels the absurd, if only on occasion. But feeling needs augmentation if the absurd is to be fully perceived or confronted. The mind must join the senses if the absurd is to be recognized and assessed. Cognizance of the absurd comes from awareness, that two-eyed look at one's self in the midst of the world's phenomena. Awareness of the absurd brings recognition of its parts. The absurd comes from the interaction between a human and the universe—and the divorce which marks the coupling.

The universe is not absurd in itself, it is simply incomprehensible. It does not yield its meaning to humans. Nor are humans absurd in themselves. They are simply concerned to know. The absurd springs from the confrontation of humans and the universe. Humans yearn to know and the universe is unfathomable: humans have nostalgia and the world is irrational. When these factors are recognized, the recognizer is aware of the absurd.

Beyond awareness comes the maintenance of the absurd. Both factors, nostalgia and the irrational, are to be sustained. The two held together create the tension of the absurd stance.

The sustenance of both might be called "lucidity," though Camus did not specifically so apply the term. But, in spite of his reference to the absurd as an "intellectual malady," Camus saw positive benefit in the awareness and acknowledgement of both nostalgia and the irrational. His own life, as we have seen, taught him about both. Furthermore, "lucidity" and "irony" were affirmative words for Camus. So, it may be right to say that the reverse—and positive—side of the absurd stance can be called "lucidity." Lucidity balances the urge of nostalgia and the acknowledgement of the irrational.

But Camus speaks of the absurd stance in *The Myth*, and shows nostalgia and the irrational in tension rather than in balance. The quest for knowing and the confession of the irrational comprise a tension from which, Camus says, a strange happiness comes. That happiness issues, he implies, from the consequences of the absurd stance: quantity, freedom, and revolt—all three closely linked.

Since ultimate meaning is not knowable—though the absurd person does not turn away from the quest for knowing—life lacks purpose. Consequently, experience is elevated. What counts is experience, the more the better. Quantity is imperative. There is no difference between one act and another if there is no ultimate meaning. The most, and not the best, is the one criterion. The amount and number of experiences are the only desirables. Piling up, amassing experience will give the fullest life.

Quantity—sometimes also referred to as "passion" or "diversity" by Camus—provides the only quality in such an undertaking. Quantity is perceived as the first good when life is meaningless. A life full of acts is the life to be realized. Hesitation produced by trying to make judgment between possible acts reduces the number of acts—and this is tantamount to reducing life. The passion for life, the grasping of all opportunities for experience, the diversity of living the fullest possible life (every moment filled with experiencing): all come as one consequence of the absurd stance.

Along with quantity is freedom, its companion. For, freed of concern for quality—a concern lifted up by moral codes, religions, and ethical systems—the potential of experience is vastly multiplied, because the absurd person is free of belief that the quality of one's acts are of significance. Without ultimate meaning, action has no bound or barrier. There are no rules for living. Everything is permitted. The most, not the best, is what counts. And freedom allows for that most.

Along with quantity and freedom comes the consequence of revolt. Revolt may be against those people or systems which impose restraints on the individual. It may be against the universal scheme of things which decrees that humans suffer and die. Though revolt often has social dimensions, it is metaphysical at heart, since it relates basically to the irrational, the meaninglessness of the universe. Nostalgia is, after all, forever frustrated by the eternal persistence of the irrational.

Social revolt is raised against governments, systems, philosophies, and religions which presume to create order out of the disorderliness in the universe. Therefore, the social rebel is necessarily also a metaphysical rebel, though he may not know it. The absurd person is in revolt against the universal scheme of things—and against those who presume to explain, to defend or to ameliorate the features of that scheme.

Socially or metaphysically focused, passively or actively exemplified, revolt is the constant characteristic of the absurd person. Though Camus does not rank the three consequences, of the three revolt seems the most closely linked to the basic equation, since both nostalgia and the irrational may provide cause for revolt, whether directly or indirectly. On the other hand, freedom and quantity may be reduced by exhaustive involvement in revolt. At any rate, given Camus's later featuring of revolt (modified into "rebellion") in *The Rebel*, it is more persistent than the other two.

Once the absurd had been defined and explicated, Camus presented instances of the absurd person, who may be taken as representative of the "strange happiness" of which he spoke. He warns that these are not examples—they are instances only.

Don Juan, pursuer and lover of women, manifests quantity and passion predominantly, of course, but his awareness of the scheme of things leads him to practice the freedom which that awareness grants—to dare rebelling against social and religious conventions.

The actor, rebelling against the confinement of living one life, lives multiple lives—lives begun, developed, and concluded in a few brief hours—with the freedom and passion which the absurd stance allows.

The conqueror, defying the humane virtues of compassion and consideration, free and disdainful of sympathy, extends his power over a multiplicity of domains for no other reason than to fill life with experience.

Having introduced these instances, Camus maintains that the lowliest clerk (Meursault of *The Stranger* is a clerk) may also sustain the absurd, and may enjoy the happiness which is linked with the absurd. He is among the "sons of the same earth . . . inseparable." He can live freely, in revolt against all constraining circumstances, passionately participating in whatever experience is available to him. So, also, can all others The absurd stance can be assumed by any and all who are lucid and aware, all who are free of the restrictions imposed by the "meaning" propounded in philosophies and religions. The absurd life is experiencing whatever comes to hand.

Camus's treatment of the absurd is straight and persuasive. It has the tone of advocacy, the ring of belief. The absurd stance is presented as response to the "one philosophical question—that of suicide." The absurd is linked with happiness—that universal goal of humans. And Sisyphus—of the title—is the heady symbol of the absurd, the prime figure of the absurd stance. Sisyphus carries the banner of happiness.

Clearly, Sisyphus is a metaphysical rebel. He is in rebellion against the gods. Condemned to death by them, because of infractions of their imposed order, Sisyphus is ordered to descend into the underworld. But he refuses that exile from living. He sallies forth into life again, and lucidly accepts the punishment of absurdity: his condemnation to fetch an ever-descending rock and push it, again and again, up the hill. But he surmounts the punishment, scorns the torment, and, face against the rock, revels in his ascendancy over his destiny. In the moments of surcease from the heaving struggle, he triumphs again and again. In the descent into the lair of the gods—where again lies the eternal rock of his condemnation—he smiles at the punishment which has not destroyed him. In that slow descent, he surveys the mineral-filled mountain and realizes that he is happy. His meaning is in his living. And in that living he is scornfully happy, superior to the gods who would impose grim life on him.

Though Camus never says so, *The Myth* and *The Stranger* appear to relate as explication and exemplification of the absurd. The two works were in process at the same time. Sisyphus, not Meursault, is the paradigm, and he is fully formed when presented. Meursault, on the other hand, the protagonist in a novel, is developed into a man of the absurd. He moves from passive, unfocused strangeness into conscious absurdity, at first only sensing the absurd. As life impinges upon him he becomes fully aware, and changes into a conscious, articulate, energetic exponent of the absurd.

Meursault is attractive to a reader, it seems, because he imbibes the inconsequential details of life, living every moment in rapt attention to the immediate. For him, satisfaction comes in the present, which is gratifying in itself, even though the days follow one another in monotonous succession. He responds to the proximate and is particularly adept at extracting nectar from the unpromising blossoms near at hand.

Yet, he is strange. Fixed on the present, anticipation has no appeal. He shuns advancement in the offer of a job transfer to Paris, without reason given. He sees no point in marrying Marie Cardona, though she obviously pleases him. Future-oriented opportunity simply exerts no attraction.

When Meursault fails to fulfill the expected ritual niceties at his mother's funeral, the reader may empathize and yet admit that he is an odd mourner. Marie Cardona remarks the strange ease with which Meursault shrugs off some things: his mourning band, the hurts of the Arab girl, Marie's own desire that they marry. The reader, attracted by his honesty, his guilelessness, his transparency, must flinch a little at his insensitivity.

Camus employs deliberate ambiguity in the description of the killing of the Arab. The searing stare of the sun, the sweat on Meursault's forehead, the throbbing of his head, the blows of light upon his eyes, the shimmering heat waves between him and the Arab—all seem to conspire to press the trigger for him. When the glittering blade reflects its flash into his eyes, the trigger yields, the butt jogs his palm, and death spits forward. The Arab is a distant threat no more.

Meursault's own telling of the fatal confrontation makes nothing of the fact that the Arab had cause for fearing him. With ten yards separating the two, the Arab's knife is no match for Meursault's revolver. Meursault's complete indifference to the plight of the Arab shows his complete solitariness. He is a stranger to the other man's humanity. He shows no concern that a man might die. He is only the forward-lurching seeker of the moment's shade. Then there is a dead man. The sun-struck Meursault, however, sees the dead body only as a panel which resounds to four raps on the door of his undoing. There is not even a "poor bastard" for the Arab.

Meursault was abused by the sun and the heat and the other converging elements. But he had put himself in the way of assault. He fated himself. Believing that it didn't matter one way or the other, Meursault turned one way rather than the other when elementary wisdom pointed in the opposite direction. With the same imprudence Meursault took one step nearer to his fallen foe to fire four more rounds into the lifeless body. It was those four, not the first shot, which Meursault recognized as the loud, fateful raps on the door of his undoing.

After the killing, Meursault shows not the slightest sign of remorse over having killed a man. His thought dwells exclusively on the responses of others to him. He laments his prison deprivations and the absence of his little joys. Not once does he show regret that he has taken a life. So Meursault continues to exhibit his almost total lack of concern for the quality of his acts. He acted—and reflected—without thought for discriminating between just and unjust acts, without attention to other than self-serving values.

The misdirected attention of the people officially relating to Meursault obscures the fact that Meursault is definitely culpable of a criminal act. His unarticulated nihilism expressed itself in indiscriminate acts, for he thought "it all comes to the same thing." He was capable of distinguishing—his admonitions to Raymond on the beach testify to this—but he saw no point in it. When his pointless actions climaxed in the death of a man,

Meursault saw nothing of the man's death quiver—but only the beginning of his own undoing. Meursault committed a gratuitous act, and walked away from it as if it were nothing but prelude to a trying time for himself.

Meursault has been depicted as a victim of circumstances: the stubborn presence of the Arab, the concatenation of assaults on his senses, the blinding light and heat of the sun. Yet he put himself in the way of destiny, he shrugged his decisions, he walked into closer and closer proximity to peril. His exclusive attention to the immediate, his preoccupation with quantity, and his concentration on himself—all led to the confrontation with the Arab and the firing of the four final shots.

The story of *The Stranger* is a history of an absurd man. He fits most of the characteristics set forth in *The Myth*. It is as if the advocacy of that book had been accepted by the character of the novel. He lacks only a cause for his defiance.

At first his rebellion is no more than reaction to laughable judicial practices. He is irritated by the flawed indictment and the conduct of the prosecution. But that irritation turns into authentic anger and rebellion when the chaplain offers his version of life's meaning. From that moment on, Meursault is a consciously absurd man. He more nearly approximates Sisyphus, though the rebellion of Meursault is less justified. After all, Meursault has committed a brutal crime.

Camus's carefully ambiguous description of the sun's effect on the shooting leads some readers to believe that Meursault is a victim. But of what? Forces outside and around him which conspire against him? A determined force of nature against which he is powerless? Meursault himself draws no such conclusion, although his description of the beach sequence uses some words suggestive of a kind of determinism. Yet he neither defends himself by claiming a "seizure" on the beach nor reflects, later, on such a "possession." Meursault hardly gives the beach episode a second thought. The consequence—his "undoing"—was the only thing of significance to him.

Those who deal with Meursault after the killing over-react just enough to his strangeness to make him seem picked-on, a naïf, a victim of the system. The examining magistrate and the defense lawyer represent that justice system which eventually produces the right verdict for the wrong reasons. But Meursault contributes to his own condemnation—he does nothing to claim self-defense, his only hope for acquittal. Nor does he pressure his court-appointed lawyer to resist the bullying tactics of the prosecution.

The same marvelous skill with which Camus described the killing of the Arab produces the same effect of ambiguity at the trial. Almost a caricature, the trial is just believable enough to create reader sympathy for Meursault while calling in question a system which ambles into spurious judgment.

Indeed, Camus may here be slyly attacking the vagaries of the propositional thinking regularly employed by practitioners of the law. He has said that irony in his work has been largely overlooked.

Meursault is put on trial in *The Stranger*. So, also, is the absurd life. There is something wrong with a man who kills and suffers no remorse, who gives only the slightest indications of solidarity with any other human. Meursault's long introspection in prison is a lengthy dwelling on himself, without a trace of recognition that both he and the dead Arab are parts of the same humanity.

Meursault honored only quantity, refused to choose between acts. Truly—admirably so—he enjoyed inconsequential things, affirming in prison that he could live in the cleft of a tree, content with observing whatever came within his line of vision. But Meursault shows the impossibility of living a hermit life within the midst of people. Unwilling to choose between acts, he finds a whole society aligned against him. He is judged to be a stranger, condemned to be alone, exiled from the community of those who also face the absurd. It is Meursault's essential self-focus, fully within the perimeter of the absurd, which casts doubt on the commendability of the absurd life. Where, after all, has it gotten Meursault? By his own actions, all consonant with the absurd stance, he has conveyed himself into a cell where experience—that be-all for Meursault—is severely strictured and limited. Jean-Paul Sartre was right when he said, "*The Stranger* is a classic work, an orderly work, written about the absurd and against the absurd."

The doubt-casting on the absurd is even more pronounced in the play *Caligula*, for Caligula, unlike Meursault, shares the heroic proportions of Sisyphus. As emperor he is free to exercise full freedom, to fulfill the passion for multiplicity of experience. Since he is the emperor, his revolt is against the universal scheme of things—and against traditions of the ruler—and not against the ruler. He, like Meursault and Sisyphus, is precipitated into the absurd by death. Caligula's sister and mistress, Drusilla, dies suddenly, and he leaps into active revolt against the scheme of things. "Men die," he says, "and they are not happy."

Previously a model emperor, Caligula becomes scourge, famine, and capriciousness in imperial clothes. During three years of revolt against the scheme of things, manifesting the absurd response to the irrational, he sculpts the absurd in his own self, His freedom is virtually unlimited. So he overturns his own reputation and upends moral standards by reversing them—rewarding those who excel at brothel patronage, using patrician wives for his own instant conjugality, ordering executions on an impulse, killing on a whim. His emperorship provides the freedom; his plural appetites issue in limitless, unqualified acts.

His revolt is necessarily metaphysical, since he is himself the social and political power. He does revolt against the traditional deportment of an emperor, rebelling, thus, against himself. But his revolt is basically against the universal scheme of things. He usurps the capriciousness attributed to the gods by fulfilling his every wish and fancy. He parodies God by bringing about famine, death, and those undeserved punishments which humans call acts of God. He requires his lords to participate in a litany to Venus, with himself posing as Venus. He exercises God's mercy and grace by destroying the incriminating tablet which establishes Cherea's guilt of conspiracy. As a final act of revolt, he exercises the prerogative of self-sacrifice—smashing his image in the mirror, setting himself up for immolation at the hands of Cherea and the patricians. Caligula rebelled against the scheme of things by creating his own irrational order.

But that was not enough. He wanted the impossible to be possible. He wanted the moon, that other-worldly luminosity. He wanted it brought to him, made his own, tucked into bed for a lovers' consummation. The moon is a symbol of his lost love, Drusilla, and of nostalgia.

Caligula and the moon convey a marvelous symbolization of the human reach for clarity outside and beyond the world. Caligula contends that the world is unsatisfactory, that it provides no meaning in spite of the human demand for meaning. If the meaning essential to happiness is not discoverable here, it must be sought elsewhere. The moon, floating nearby, but distant from any reaching arms; regularly withdrawing and disguising herself in darkness, but periodically drifting closer— that moon captivates Caligula.

The unreachable moon, Caligula concludes, is the one consort who could satisfy his nostalgia. He reaches for her himself, but he also deputizes another to snare the moon for him, to entice the moon into intimacy, to cast a net skyward and haul her in for Caligula, to be the matchmaker—Hélicon is chosen to search out and seize the unseizable. Hélicon personifies Caligula's yearning for meaning.

In the earliest versions of *Caligula*, Hélicon is a minor character, without the full dimensions of a person. But in the version which Camus staged at the Chateau d'Angers late in his life, the character of Hélicon was amplified, given more attention, given more prominence. Thus, what is only implicit in the early version, is made explicit: Caligula's concern for nostalgia is incarnated in a full-blown Hélicon. It is deeply significant that in this final version, directed by Camus himself, Hélicon is killed, along with Caligula, after shouting a warning to Caligula to save himself. That outcome was another way for Camus to say that there is great danger in yielding fully to nostalgia.

Caligula represents the fully developed absurd man. He demonstrates, concurrently, the yearning of nostalgia and the recognizing of the irrational. As emperor he is fully free to exercise his freedom—there are no constraints—and to amass great quantities of experience. And his whole deportment is revolt against expectations, against traditions, against moral codes, against the very scheme of things. He is the consummate absurd man.

But as a man Caligula does not measure up to Sisyphus, for he gives up on life, as Sisyphus does not. Sisyphus refuses the underworld exile decreed by the gods and returns to life in its fullness, even with the punishment which that entails. Caligula, on the other hand, driven to distraction and madness by the death of Drusilla, contrives a complex suicide by forcing others to do away with him.

Camus's primary question in *The Myth* was, "Should one kill oneself?" The answer is "no," because life is worth living. Yet Caligula, the personification of the absurd man, finally admitting that he has chosen the wrong freedom, concocts a superior suicide. Caligula does not commend the absurd.

Caligula is Camus's rebellion against the philosophy of the absurd delineated in *The Myth of Sisyphus*. All the consequences of the absurd—freedom, quantity, and revolt—are given free rein in *Caligula*. The emperor, unlike Meursault, is as unrestricted as a man can be. He fully actualizes the absurd consequences.

But Caligula—unlike the solitary individual Meursault—is surrounded by people dependent upon him, related to him in various ways. Though he is supreme, Caligula operates within the social setting. His immense freedom is thoroughly obtrusive. His excesses impinged on the lives of others. The patricians, despite their posturings of allegiance and loyalty, realized, early on, that they must do something to curb the full expression of Caligula's absurdity. He is finally called into account.

Caligula and his unlimited freedom creates Cherea. Cherea epitomizes opposition to Caligula's untrammeled freedom. Rebellion springs up against the inevitable excesses of total freedom. Cherea challenges the dominance of freedom and quantity when he says, "I believe there are actions which are better than others," (contrary to Meursault's assertion that "one might fire, or not fire—and it would come to absolutely the same thing.")

Cherea also expresses a theme which will be prominent in *The Plague*, when he says, "to live, and to be happy" are worthy goals. "Neither, to my mind, is possible if one pushes the absurd to its logical conclusions. As you see, I'm quite an ordinary sort of man. True, there are moments when, to feel free of them, I desire the death of those I love, or I hanker after women from whom the ties of family or friendship debar me. Were logic everything, I'd kill or fornicate on such occasions; but I consider that these passing fancies have no great importance. If everyone set to gratifying them, the world would be impossible to live in, and happiness, too, would go by the board."

Freedom is not an unqualified desirable. One freedom is better than another. Caligula had exercised the wrong freedom. So there is no unlimited freedom, there is no unconditional freedom, there is no total freedom. Freedom as a consequence of the absurd is not the absolute it first appeared to be.

Cherea incarnates that resistance which constitutes Camus's veritable disclaimer of the absurd. Cherea is the carrier of the same rebellious thought manifested in the interplay between *The Stranger*, *The Myth of Sisyphus*, and *Caligula*. The acts and words of Cherea foreshadow the thought Camus would develop in *The Rebel*.

Camus wrote *Caligula*, *The Myth*, and *The Stranger* in the same period of time—concurrently. The negatives, in other words, were underway while—perhaps even before—he wrote his explication of the absurd in *The Myth*. The attacks against the possibility of living the absurd accompanied the apparent advocacy of the absurd.

The interplay of the works shows rebellious thought turning on itself. Camus's thought, in contrast with propositional thinking, led him elsewhere, somewhere beyond the absurd, while he presented the absurd. Furthermore, "Even as I was writing *The Myth of Sisyphus* I was thinking about the essay on revolt that I would write later on, in which I would attempt, after having described the different aspects of the feeling of the Absurd, to describe the different attitudes of man in revolt."

Camus objected to the "modern mania of identifying the author with his subject matter" and to his being considered a prophet of the absurd. "Yet, what else have I done except reason about an idea I discovered in the streets of my time? That I have nourished this idea (and part of me nourishes it still) along with my whole generation goes without saying. I simply set it far enough away so that I could deal with it and decide on its logic."

Camus's method is to give an idea its head, to follow that idea as it works itself out, to decide on its logic, to pursue it on its own terms—all while recognizing that, since the universe is irremediably irrational, beyond the understanding of humans, nothing is final. Become the proponent of an idea, if only for a time, give it free rein, let it run, watch it, test it, discover its truths and its falsities. Rebellious thought will display its mettle, its viability, its life-serving qualities, if any.

In this period Camus's thought concentrated on the absurd. But that concentration never featured straight-line development. The thought extended itself critically, drawing implications to their extremities, supportable or non-supportable, reversing or truncating the well-turned thought which might arise. Thus, *Caligula* seriously undercuts what *The Myth* supports. By drawing out all its eventuations the viability of living the absurd is put to the test.

Camus wrote these three works concurrently. Whatever the sequence, *The Myth of Sisyphus* sets forth a cohesive philosophy while *The Stranger* and *Caligula*, setting that theory in life, show that it has serious, fatal flaws. Furthermore, according to Olivier Todd, he and his supporters wanted the three works to come out "one on top of the other."

Eschewing the supportive buttressing of the mode which logical thinking employs, Camus engages his works in interaction and opposition, displaying the rebellious feature which marks his thought.

IV

Remnants and Rebels

Though Camus rejected the absurd in general, a substantial part of it remained. The surviving remnants, after the experiential testing of *The Stranger* and *Caligula*, are discernible in his later writings.

Nostalgia and the irrational, set out in *The Myth of Sisyphus*, appear prominently in later works. Characters display them, alone or together, sometimes subtly, sometimes openly. Sole focus on nostalgia results in social imposition; single focus on the irrational issues in behavior excess. But the two-eyed mode of seeing, with one eye on nostalgia and one eye on the irrational, is repeatedly commended. This binocular mode may be called "lucidity": the discipline of attending to both at once, as in the yoking and valuing of opposites in *l'Envers et l'Endroit*.

The irrational, nostalgia, and revolt, one of the named consequences of the absurd, all receive continued attention, with revolt undergoing considerable refinement. But the cohesive totality of the absurd stance is set aside. That stance was exercised in *The Stranger* and *Caligula*, and led its practitioners to confinement and destruction, revealing the un-viability of the absurd life. The absurd consequences of freedom and quantity do not survive that testing. But revolt, the third consequence, does survive.

Revolt appeared in the characters of Meursault and Caligula. In *The Stranger* the revolt of Meursault endures, despite his imprisonment, and elicits the reader's admiration. But in *Caligula*, revolt is clouded by virtue of the fact that Caligula—both emperor and de facto god—was in revolt against himself. His revolt was singular, unrepeatable, its import ambiguous and non-definitive. But neither Meursault nor Caligula was to be the last Camusian character to manifest revolt. Revolt comes to the forefront in Camus's next offerings.

Camus starts his exploration of revolt and rebellion by focusing on characters in revolt. A play, *The Misunderstanding*, begins the investigation. It is set in the region which had depressed Camus markedly during the visit described in Chapter 2. The plot was suggested by a news clipping which Camus found there in a hotel room—and the finding of such a clipping was made a part of Meursault's story in *The Stranger*.

Martha, the principal character in the play, feels exiled in her Central European homeland. She rails at the life she has to live, encircled by gloomy hills. An inn-keeper, feeling trapped in her dreary circumstances, she revolts against her confinement.

Though neither an emperor nor a clerk, Martha is as driven as Caligula, as self-centered as Meursault. Intent on escaping her exile, without constraint of morality or compassion, she acts to escape her confinement and realize her ambition to live on the Mediterranean, in the land of the sea and the sun.

So obsessed is she with achieving her goal that she devises a murderous scheme to gain that brighter land and enlists her mother in the operation. The two prey upon patrons of their small hotel, choosing solitary men carrying large sums of money as their victims.

Jan, Martha's brother, appears at the inn, incognito, a solitary, money-laden man. Against the tearful advice of his wife

Maria, he has arranged a surprise for the mother and the sister he left behind some twenty years before.

He has a beautiful wife, a successful business, a residence in the land of the sea and the sun. Now rich, he returns to his family, who know nothing of his success or of his whereabouts. Having created his own particular and satisfactory order, he intends to share his good fortune with his mother and his sister. He becomes a guest of the inn.

As his wife points out, all Jan need do is present himself to his family and offer the better life he is anxious to give them. But he wants to re-acquaint himself with his family without revealing his identity. His is the naiveté of innocence.

He is a captive of nostalgia. Since life has gone well for him, he can't imagine how badly it can go for others. Nor does it occur to him that his anonymity might reveal unpleasant things. His wife tries to impress him with the potential for disappointment. But he laughs off her fears, assuring her that all will be well. She, aware of the reality of the irrational, as he is not, finally leaves him to his unreasonable adventure.

Martha and her mother, unaware of Jan's identity, resolve to make Jan the last contributor to Martha's goal. The mother has vague misgivings about the venture this time, and almost aborts it. But they execute the plan. They manage to drug their guest and carry him, unconscious, to the river, where he is carried out of sight by the current.

By chance, back at the hotel, Jan's passport is discovered. The women then realize what they've done. Anguished over this crime against her own son, the mother drowns herself in the river even then silting over his body.

Martha, his sister, and Maria, his wife, introduced to one another by the death of Jan, confront one another in passionate argument. One speaks bitterly of her deprived life, the other mourns the intolerable loss of the man whose life she had shared. Martha expresses her gospel of bitter news and Maria plaintively utters a distraught call for God's mercy.

Maria, a minor character, is the only one with any chance of eliciting spectator sympathy. Yet for this victim of a man's stupid naiveté and a woman's rapacity, there is no rescue. No one can extricate Maria from such a skewed, human-made scheme of things. Anticipation unrealized, happiness shattered—these are two different effects of the same malady. "Men die, and they are not happy," said Caligula.

In the final scene of the play, Maria, crying out for help, seems to be appealing to God. But it is the old manservant, ambling across the stage, who answers her. He, a symbol of unwillingness or inability to deliver anyone from primal suffering, gives the only response she will hear. His single word reply, "No," is the final line of the play.

Critics point out the shortcomings of *The Misunderstanding* as a play. The plot revolves around mistaken identity; there are an excessive number of too-convenient entrances and exits; an accidental glance at Jan's passport reveals his identity, too late to avert the tragedy. It is a flawed play—but the larger problem is that playgoers found it difficult to sympathize with Martha, the principal character. Meursault of *The Stranger*, also faulted in character, wins much sympathy from readers. Martha does not.

Martha feels herself exiled in the interior of Europe—as did Camus, then in the central mountains of France for treatment of his recurrent tuberculosis. Martha and her creator both yearned for the sea and the sun of the Mediterranean. But Martha is totally devoted to her singularity, evincing no semblance of solidarity with others, even her mother. Her hardness, her singlemindedness, her manipulation of her mother, her coldbloodedness commend her to no one; and all combine to make her seem deserving of exile. Her only ultimate is pity for herself. Driven by nothing worse than unpleasant surroundings, she is willing to kill repeatedly in order to extricate herself. So when she leaves to make rendezvous in the river with her mother and her brother, the spectator feels less sorrow for her than for the unknown deceased in a passing funeral procession.

The mother, certainly a more sympathetic character, nevertheless participates in murder for a daughter undeserving of such singular motherly devotion. Jan, the son and brother, is a potentially sympathetic character, but he stupidly insists on playing the game of incognito.

Most characters lack elemental wisdom or goodness—Jan plays the romantic, his sister and mother commit capital crimes, the old manservant refuses even a semblance of consolation for Maria. Maria, the wife, who gave the altogether sensible warnings about her husband's plan—and who stood up against Martha's invective—is the only sympathetic personage of the play.

The absurd man, Camus had said, knew a strange kind of happiness. And happiness is the engine of this strange play. Action in it is prompted by the quest of happiness though the play is filled with gloom. Martha rants against her lack of happiness and the scheme of things which presses her between the dark and somber hills far from the sea and the sun where she believes that happiness abides. But Maria's happiness is threatened and then destroyed, with relief nowhere in sight.

The mother is an accomplice in the murderous pursuit of her daughter's happiness. Jan's happiness is singular, ingenuous, and blithe, despite his work experience. Content in his possession of a pleasant life, he is happily settled in nostalgia. He expects to extend his happiness to his family.

Though not the principal character, Jan is the fulcrum of the action. He and his plan to offer pleasant life and happiness to his family precipitates the crisis, when he presents himself incognito. He does not recognize the irrational. He is neither absurd man nor rebel—he knows of nothing to rebel against. He is blissfully unaware of any fault-lines in the structure of things.

Camus admitted that the play's gloominess bothered him as much as it did the public and that "It is a very dismal image of human fate." In response to criticism of the play, he said, "Everything would have been different if the son had said: 'It is I; here is my name.' . . . in an unjust or indifferent world man can save himself, and save others, by practicing the most basic sincerity and pronouncing the most appropriate word."

But there would have been no misunderstanding—and no play—if Jan had spoken up. And, truly, Jan is little more than the bland, unwitting pawn in the plot. Furthermore, Camus's comment is strangely silent about the actions of Martha —the principal character in proportion and focus—in her brutal rebellion.

Martha has mounted an assault against the irrational accidents of life which wall her up in the mountains. She is clearly, defiantly in rebellion against her lot in the universe. In her personality Martha repeats the darkness of her surroundings. In her confinement she seeks the sun as Caligula had sought the moon. She senses the irrational in the confining mountains and yearns with nostalgia for the sea she's never seen. She carries signs of the absurd unconsciously, without awareness, yet she, of all in *The Misunderstanding*, most resembles the absurd man.

Of the three consequences of the absurd, passion is scarcely manifest in Martha. She has no passion for things at hand, but only looks toward satisfaction in that other place which she has not yet reached. She does not enjoy the givens around her. She finds nothing attractive on which to spend any passion. She is neither a Meursault nor a Sisyphus—those two who found features to enjoy in their tightly constricted lives.

However, the consequence of freedom does appear in Martha. She is free of scruples, of pity, of sentiment; she brooks no ethical questions. Her freedom from religious conviction is evidenced in the remarkably passionate scene between her and Maria. There, her rebellion against religious doctrine matches—or exceeds—her freedom from it. For, though Maria exhibits an authentic Christian faith, in the interchange between the two, it is Martha who is the evangelist. Maria, stricken with the theft of life, can now do nothing more than cry for help and relief from God in her time of sorrow and need. But Martha, free of pity, spews out a demand for Maria to accept Martha's bitter faith, a faith which she describes as faithful to God, since God is hard and silent as stone in the face of human sufferings. Martha thus engages in metaphysical revolt.

Revolt is Martha's dominant characteristic. Intent on extricating herself from the grip of the irrational, she adopts the irrational herself, willingly imposing death, the extreme form of the irrational. She operates on the premise that one act is as good as another, with murder an act of little significance. In absurd terms, to satisfy her nostalgia, she has yielded to the irrational by employing its means.

Martha shows the dark side of revolt, in exemplifying the negative aspects of the absurd. She, willing to do anything to achieve her own ends, shows no happiness, but only its lack, although *The Myth* linked happiness and the absurd. Not as heroic as Sisyphus, nor as ingenuous as Meursault, nor as violently tragic as Caligula, her life and attitudes are no more suasive for rebellion than were the others for the absurd.

Martha's dominant characteristic is revolt, one of the consequences of the absurd. She manifestly incarnates revolt. She rebels against her environment, her place in life, and the ordinary human virtues. But her revolt has nothing to commend it. It is entirely self-centered and unscrupulous. It reveals none of revolt's positive qualities and carries only the negative attributes of revolt. Her revolt matches the darkness of her exile.

The true rebel, as will be seen, rebels for humankind. That cannot be said of Martha. In her revolt she oppresses others who have nothing whatever to do with her exile. She rebels for herself, not for humanity. She does not exhibit solidarity. Yet Martha is more rebel than absurd woman, since she lacks passion and any sense of happiness in the present. Set against the admirable rebels who follow in the Camusian corpus, she must be considered an anti-rebel.

The series on rebellion, as did the sequence on the absurd, began with the negative. As the negative instance of Caligula was developed before the less offensive Meursault and the admirable Sisyphus, so the procession of rebels starts with the brooding, dark, vituperative Martha. The series will culminate with the lyrical, fastidious Kaliayev and Dora of *The Just Assassins*, Camus's last play. Between these are the multiple rebels of *The Plague*, a novel.

The philosophical groundings beneath *The Plague* were set out in *The Myth*. The extensive, analytical probing of rebellion, and its distinction from revolution, was to come in *The Rebel*. Between the two essays, methodologically if not strictly chronologically, were two plays, *Caligula* and *The Misunderstanding*, and two novels, *The Stranger* and *The Plague*.

Although linear thinking would present the characters of a novel as practical examples of theory in practice, the personages in *The Plague* prove no case, though there is rapport with the thought of the two essays.

Oran, a happy city, is the setting of *The Plague*. In the novel, the city's complacency is upset by a visitation of plague. The city seems no more qualified than others for the testing which issues from the epidemic, though Father Paneloux, at first, asserts that appropriateness.

Complacent and at ease in pleasant circumstances, citizens at first ignore the evidences around them. They are unwilling to accept the conclusion that they are threatened with plague. But it soon becomes undeniable—the city is plague-stricken.

At the very beginning of the novel, without any warning, rats, some diseased, some dead, are suddenly discovered. Initially, people attach no significance to the appearance of the rats, denying or overlooking any import in the event. When the phenomenon can no longer be ignored, however, the people blame one another for the trouble which has stricken the happy city. The evidence of swollen and distorted rats, together with human illnesses which have remarkable similarity to plague, finally bring a most reluctant city administration to declare a state of siege. In the testing, various human responses arise, some uncomely, some despicable, some heroic.

The narrator of *The Plague* tells his readers that, if any are to be considered heroes, one of them is surely Joseph Grand. Otherwise small-dimensioned, he is grand in his name and in his spirit. He works for the government, as a minor clerk, in an insignificant job with commensurate pay. He has lost his wife of several years to a more exciting man, yet he refers fondly to her and admits to loving his relatives. He has not gone sour on life.

As the plague assaults the city, Grand continues his regular duties, adding to them the chore of keeping the vital statistics of the plague's deadly progress. Thus he does his part to fight against the irrational. Still, he manages to find joy, through the little pleasures available to him. After-hours he seeks the perfect sentence with which to open the long-considered first paragraph of a fancied novel. His room is filled with pages of discarded attempts—to achieve the perfect unity and clarity needed to express his meaning. His nostalgia is clearly and humorously evidenced by this passionate goal of creating a novel which will bring the acclaim of a great "Hats off!"

Joseph Grand thus exhibits features of the absurd man: He recognizes the irrational, yet he does not yield to it, but fights it; and he honors nostalgia by his belief in the possibility of novelistic success. Like the absurd man, he engages in revolt against the arbitrariness of life. But, unlike the absurd man, he neither indulges in the extravagance of quantity nor flaunts the excesses of freedom. He is a moderate who also deviates from the absurd in another notable way—other people, even his absented wife, are truly important to him.

Grand is an ordinary man. He joins the resistance to the plague more out of basic decency than anything else. There are no heroics with him. He articulates no defiance of the gods. He is a quiet devotee of life who has been hurt by it—and he fights against that which hurts others. Through it all, he is soberly happy. When he, too, is stricken with plague, he is the first to survive its assault. Grand, in his small way, is the precursor of the rebel—not the revolutionary—later detailed in *The Rebel.*

Cottard is something else. Totally self-absorbed, he finds himself singularly at home in the context of the plague. Before the plague, some crime had put the police on his trail. Life treated him so badly that he attempted suicide. He was found hanging behind a door on which he had chalked the words, "Come in, I've just hanged myself." Rescued, he finds new life in the dominion of the plague. Hard times do for him what good times could not do.

With the coming of the plague, Cottard becomes only one of the many who are now also under threat. He's relieved of concern that the police will track him down. He basks in the protection of the plague, glorying in the fact that no one is now safe from punishment. He's joined by others who are also wanted men.

The termination of the plague, after its long siege, is bad news for Cottard, though other citizens welcome the possibility of a happy life. For him, the threat of apprehension is renewed. After a brief meeting with some questioning strangers—thought to be the police—he barricades himself in his rooms. From his window he fires wildly at the people who are celebrating the departure of the plague and their release. He is enraged that normal times are following the defeat of the scourge, for he'll be a wanted man again.

With the characters of Grand and Cottard Camus reconnoiters the qualities of the rebel. Grand's is a focus-less rebellion, quiet and tempered, a way of coping with the hard realities of his life. As Meursault was unreflective, so is Grand. But Grand is not a stranger. He is one with the people. His rebellion, below the level of consciousness, under the plane of awareness, instinctually rises out of his feeling of solidarity with all afflicted by the plague. Yet, the narrator tells the reader, he is a hero if there are any. The common man, like Grand, motivated by his basic humanity, can rebel against his fate and be his own hero.

But Cottard, at odds with humanity, does not revolt against the plague. He becomes a part of that oppressive movement which makes humans suffer and die. No longer the only one pursued, he revels in a new, strange freedom. His happiness comes from the world's unhappiness. He is in counter-revolt, with the basic wish that others may fail in their resistance to the forces oppressing them. Cottard's response shows him to be the contrary of the rebel.

Rieux, the physician, is central to the story, the chief personage of *The Plague.* As a physician, Rieux is acquainted with those who act in the crisis. Like Grand and Rambert, he is alone, his wife kept out of the city by the quarantine, so the doctor gives even more than undivided attention to his resistance. Without home responsibilities, Rieux is totally absorbed with the irrational. The "scheme of things" (Rieux's oft-repeated phrase) elicits his dogged and energetic opposition. He is in metaphysical revolt.

In contrast with Grand, Rieux is largely one-dimensioned. In his struggle against the plague, Rieux is held like a wrestler in constant embrace with the irrational, while Grand honors nostalgia with something outside and beyond the plague—his novel and the search for its immortal first line. Truly, Dr. Rieux may be less one-dimensional than his actions suggest, since he is the chronicler of the events recounted in *The Plague*. But knowledge of this identity comes to the reader exceedingly late in the book, the late disclosure constituting a breach of authorial etiquette. In the story as told up to the end, Rieux is thoroughly concentrated on the plague, the irrational, and the force behind both.

As a physician, Rieux is necessarily involved, but his participation goes beyond basic duty. There are two possibilities for responding to this world, he tells the Priest, Father Paneloux: "A man can't cure and know at the same time. So let's cure as quickly as we can. That's the more urgent job." So he fights the plague, intervening as he is able, seeing people through illness, interrupting suffering, putting off death, resisting the very order of things.

Rieux's choice of profession came from a basic motivation, then intensified by the plague. He chose medicine to confront the scheme of things, to save some victims, to oppose the irrationalities of pain and death. For him, patients are symbols of a vast disorder in the universe, a faulted regime which consigns humans to misery and demise. His all-encompassing attention to that disorder separates him from the other dimensions of life.

But Rieux does not press his views on other people. He urges Rambert to pursue his own happiness, saying that such pursuit is not dishonorable. Only occasionally, however, is there a hint or glimpse in Rieux of anything other than his focus on the disorder of the plague.

Rieux has allowed the irrational to define him. He has no time for joys or pleasures. His is a heroic role, played at the cost of some of his self. In recording the chronicle of the plague and talking with Tarrou, he may have been led toward lucidity, that two-eyed way of looking at life. And he was occasionally drawn by Tarrou back into the fuller life, the two once enjoying a swim in the sea. But his concentration was on his fight against the plague.

Tarrou lives a life of observation and engagement. He jots notes about the idiosyncratic behavior of people under the onslaught. He questions himself and others about the living of life, about facing disorder, about the possibility of sainthood without God. For him, philosophical questions have large significance. He lives life reflectively, wanting to know. He honors his nostalgia.

Yet, though not his duty by vocation, Tarrou puts himself in the forefront of the city's fight against the plague. He voluntarily organizes Sanitary Squads which function alongside the professional plague-fighters. He is in conflict with the irrational, concerned to resist it, to reduce human suffering, to break the plague's hold on the people of Oran.

But Tarrou does not forfeit reflection. Fight against this physical plague does not seize his total attention. He ponders his father's vocation as a judge who, assuming the prerogative of God, sentences others to death. Tarrou sees in that the arrogant presumption of self-innocence: "because this one is judged to be guilty, I am free of guilt." By intimate acquaintance with his father's power of fatal judgment, Tarrou has become an opponent of capital punishment. But, more than that, he comes to understand that he himself is guilty of causing pain for others by his concern for himself. Without an external source of infection, Tarrou sees that he has had plague throughout his life—internal, self-generated plague.

Tarrou's rebellion, then, is both anthropological and metaphysical: against the inner promptings which put humans on the side of plague; against the outside forces which abuse humans. With his concern for curing and for knowing, he recognizes that humans are both victims and victimizers, whereas Rieux saw them only as victims. Of the two, Tarrou is the lucid one.

Tarrou's lucidity is a friendly counterpoint to the nearsighted vision of Rieux. Both watch the plague sear the deserving and the undeserving, the guilty and the innocent, the old and the young, and dispense indiscriminate mutilation. For Rieux, the source of plague, disorder, and misery is the cosmic "scheme of things," and he sees no point in giving it more thought. But Tarrou scans it with his larger vision. He notes the old man's loss of targets for spitting when cats are dispersed by the plague. He wonders whether the old asthmatic's continuous pea-by-pea transfer of dried peas from one bowl to another is a version of present-day sainthood. He seeks meaning even in the belly of the irrational. Rieux sees only wounded humanity and the blows of the wounder, but Tarrou recognizes both plague-in-the-universe and plague-within-humans. There is plague imposed from outside humanity and plague residing within—external plague and internal plague.

Father Paneloux and Raymond Rambert provide additional insights into the varieties of human response to the plague. Both articulate their responses in words and actions.

Remnants and Rebels

Father Paneloux, a Jesuit priest, initially accepts everything, since he believes that everything comes from God. His is the certainty of nostalgia. Since the plague has visited the city, it must be deserved, for the universe works out God's will. The people, Paneloux believes, have brought it down on themselves—it has not come without cause. The sinful quality of the people's lives must be that cause.

Paneloux's belief system accounts for everything. The phenomenon of the plague must fit into that system. If God directs all things, then the people deserve the chastisement. Life deeds and punishment are related. The plague punishes, therefore the people are culpable, and there is no thought of innocence.

He cannot see or admit the possibility of human suffering without any cause, or of death without justice. For he believes that everything can be known, is understandable, can be comprehended. Thus Paneloux denies the existence of the irrational. He cannot see it. The yearning of nostalgia has clouded his near vision. He is not lucid.

But Paneloux is not insensitive. And the plight of the little son of M. Othon, the magistrate, brings him into the suffering presence of innocence. In the hospital, Paneloux, along with Tarrou and Rieux, is at the bedside of the boy, ten or twelve years old, a victim of the plague. The boy is splayed out, flattened on "the bed of his crucifixion." The men stand and wait, powerless to do more than observe and sympathize. Tarrou is silent, as if to say that that's the way it is in life. Rieux, again frustrated in his role as physician, is unable to draw the boy away from this scourging death.

Paneloux is deeply perplexed. The sight of innocent death intrudes upon his theology. There is no discernible meaning in this death. As he cries out, "My God, spare this child!" he reveals the recovery of his near vision. He has become lucid.

The Myth of Sisyphus asserts that those who ascribe to a philosophy or profess a religious faith have committed philosophical suicide. Paneloux, at first, is such a "suicide." Yet Camus, his creator, grants him a rebirth. For Paneloux steps out of his role of rigid doctrinaire into a man of searching faith. Chastened by the suffering he's seen, he decides to fight against the plague—which he had believed to be deserved punishment of the people. He takes on some of Tarrou's perspective and joins in the work of the Sanitary Squads.

Two sermons illustrate Paneloux's attitudes. The first confidently blames the people for drawing the wrath of God. The second, preached after witnessing the young boy's death, comes from a changed preacher. Assurance and assertion are gone; sympathy and pity have come. No longer calling it the just punishment of God, Paneloux now sees only enigma and mystery in the plague and its visitation. He had thought that plague was within the will of God, and thus had to be endured. But innocence showed him the evil of the plague, and brought him into the ranks of those who resisted the plague's invasion.

When Father Paneloux dies, he coughs up a bit of red matter not attributable to the plague. His death is called a "doubtful case"—he has symptoms of neither bubonic nor pneumonic plague, the two types which doctors have identified. That red matter—is it no more than a symbol of the suffering permitted by God, or is it a piece of the sacramental host? Is the reader to take this "doubtful case" as a case of choking on permitted suffering—or as a case of "philosophical suicide?"

Paneloux did not give up his nostalgia. Faith in God was strong in him to the end. But he rebelled against his conception of God, when he recognized innocent suffering, when he accepted belief in innocence, when he entertained the possibility of undeserved punishment. When his eyes were opened he developed lucidity. Paneloux received a novelist's highest tribute—Camus allowed Paneloux to break out of character.

Raymond Rambert, a journalist in Oran on assignment from metropolitan France, is quarantined in the troubled city. His interactions with Dr. Rieux provide insight into the characters of both men.

With the argument that he is out of place, that Oran is not his home, Rambert pleads with the doctor for a certificate of good health so that he can leave the city. He's anxious to return to Paris and the woman he loves. But Rieux refuses. While sympathetic, the doctor argues that Rambert could be infected with the plague, even though he has no symptoms.

Yet, though Rieux fears the possibility of extending the plague outside the city, he does nothing to prevent Rambert's numerous attempts to escape, even though he might be a carrier. Rieux, who has put aside his own happiness, thus grants high value to the happiness of his friend.

The relations between the two, one a plague-wrestler, the other a happiness-seeker, provide for some of the most telling developments in the novel. Frustrated over his exile and separation from his woman in Paris, Rambert strikes out in anger. Enlisting the forces of criminality for his own benefit, he calls on Cottard and a group of smugglers to help him make repeated attempts to escape.

But when he learns from Tarrou that Rieux is also separated from his wife, who is in a sanitarium outside the city, Rambert reconsiders. So impressed is he by Rieux's calm endurance of his forced singleness that he concludes it's wrong to try to escape the plague—it is shameful to be happy by oneself. He joins Tarrou's Sanitary Squads.

Rambert, like Paneloux, had his myth. He saw the world as the site for happiness. Dismissing life close around him, he took the distant, nostalgic view, yearning for the far-away woman of his happiness. That happiness was threatened in Oran. As Rieux's goal was to beat down the plague, the eternal plague, Rambert's goal was reunion with his loved one—his happiness.

But when he saw that happiness itself—humanity's happiness—was in jeopardy, he looked again. Seeing the wounded, he saw himself. He saw the closer vision with opened eyes. He saw that he, as a member of humanity, was one of the vulnerable ones. He accepted his solidarity with them. He became lucid. He broke off with the smugglers, and then joined the fight against the plague.

The distinctions between Rambert and Rieux are definitive. Rieux, fixed on the irrational, thoroughly suppressed his happiness while fighting the plague. Rambert, driven by his nostalgia for happiness, looked past the irrational until his friend's engagement with it brought it into view. Seeing with new eyes, Rambert joined in resisting the irrational, without setting aside either his or the people's nostalgia for happiness. He became lucid. He became a rebel.

The Plague assembles a variety of rebels or near-rebels. Most are engaged in resisting the causes of human suffering. Some rebel from the beginning, some are late-enlisters. Some are blind to anything but the adversary before them. Some are so intent on distant views that the close scene is blurred. All of them recognize that people suffer and die, that people are not happy.

The scourge of the plague confronts people with an impersonal enemy, which most of them resist. Some simply oppose that which assaults them, without further thought. Some, Father Paneloux among them, look beyond the plague and are agitated by its implication. Some, Rieux among them, rail against the scheme of things which allows the plague's visitation. One, Tarrou, fulfills expectations of the rebel.

Tarrou goes beyond rebelling against the plague. Despite the attention he devotes to fighting the plague, he, like Paneloux, seeks the larger meaning of life. Both men honor nostalgia and acknowledge the irrational. But Tarrou, alone of all the characters, is drawn to look inside, to assess himself internally.

Acutely disturbed by the presence of the plague, Tarrou makes multiple response to the human condition: he seeks the meaning of life and suffering; he looks deeply inside human character; he fights the plague. His concern is not confined to the immediate, but is directed to the whole of his own life, with implications for all human beings. He is fully lucid. He is a true rebel.

Tarrou, had he been in our milieu, might have been content with condemning his father's vocation of judge, and with explaining away his own tendency to judge. But Tarrou looks inside—inside himself, and inside human character per se—and discovers plague: an inherent tendency to judge and oppress. This is not the plague of the microbe, but the plague of utter self-focus, with denial or disdain for other humans. Inner plague is the failure to acknowledge, accept, and honor human solidarity.

In one of the novel's last chapters, Tarrou tells Rieux of the conclusions he's drawn from life: "Over time, I have come to see clearly that even those who were better than others were not able to keep themselves from killing or permitting killing today, because that was the logic in which they were living. For we cannot do a thing in this world without the risk of causing death."

This warning against the danger of killing is more than a call for vigilance or for defense against calamity and catastrophe. It's also a strong plea to maintain an inner surveillance, an inner watchfulness against infecting by judging and condemning. Tarrou talks with Rieux of inner plague: "Yes, I continue to be ashamed, for I understand this—we are all under plague, and

I'm bereft of peace. I still seek that peace, trying to understand everything and being the mortal enemy of no one. I only know that I must do what is needed in order not to be a plague-carrier; and that this alone may give hope for peace, or a good death if it fails."

But this inner plague is not in Tarrou alone, he tells Rieux: "I know with certainty (yes, Rieux, I know life, you well know) that each one carries the plague within, because no one—no one in the world—is unscathed. One has to watch without blinking so as not to be led, in a moment of distraction, to breathe in the face of another and pass on the infection."

With these words Tarrou conveys a secular version of sin: Something like plague is internal; humans judge and oppress one another. "The honorable person, the one who infects hardly anyone, is the one with the least possible distraction," the one who guards against passing on the plague within.

Tarrou dies the good death of which he spoke, without finding the peace for which he'd hoped, and the novel ends with the prediction that plague will come forth again to assault a chosen city for "the bane and the enlightenment of humans." There will again be victims, and rebels, and those seeking some kind of sainthood.

A novel does not provide for systematic exposition, nor is Camus concerned to be systematic. But a line of thought can be extracted from *The Plague*: The universe is irrational; there is undeserved human suffering within it; the cause of that suffering must be opposed; pestilence maims, but in face of it humans define themselves; those who suffer are to be pitied and aided; those who resist the cause of suffering are admirable; those who seek to cure the afflicted and to search for meaning are full rebels; those who seek meaning, oppose plague, and recognize their own complicity in plague are the honorable ones, the saint-like ones.

Some critics at the time judged the novel in relation to the Occupation of France by Germany. True, the novel could be seen as an allegory: A society cut off from the world; the plague as the German occupation of France; Cottard and other profiteers in the situation as collaborators; plague fighters as members of the Resistance. Thus, Rieux was interpreted as Camus's model for resistance to the Nazis—actions taken against the plague were seen as resistance to the occupation.

This interpretation poses Rieux, the principal character, as Camus's personification of proper response in extreme circumstances. Rieux reacted to the emergency, tended to the infected, assisted the afflicted. But he did nothing to eject, evict, or cut down the enemy. From this perspective the efforts were ineffective, for the plague simply ran its course, was not driven out. His work, these critics said, was no more than that of the Red Cross. A more direct, forceful, dirty-hands response was called for, they asserted.

With the story interpreted by the touchstone of the Occupation, Rieux is seen as the principal character. But concentration on Rieux draws attention away from Tarrou, who is the more fully-formed, more complete character. And Tarrou—a non-professional who could have sat on the sidelines—steps up to challenge the plague, and volunteers to fight the plague. He organizes the Sanitary Squads and empathizes with victims of the siege, whatever their place in life. In his search for the larger meaning of the plague and life he keeps the plague diary used by the narrator. He plumbs his own depths and confesses his own complicity. He was the full-rounded rebel.

Yet this consummate rebel—along with Paneloux, who became a two-eyed surveyor of life—was assigned by his creator to die of the plague. Tarrou succumbs undefeated, but his creator has not made him a hero or a conqueror, as some might expect. This is no thesis novel. But Tarrou is a rebel of the highest order.

Camus's macro-rhetoric is discursive. It is not systematic. It attends to its subject—without the goal of "proof"—and may advance or double back on itself. Not predictable, it is not unfocused, but it is pointed. Philosophical ideas set out in *The Myth*, and later in *The Rebel*, are implicit in *The Plague*. Personages of the novel reflect or project the thought of the essays on the absurd and rebellion, but this is not a "thesis work," a type decried by Camus, for, like the bulk of his larger work, it avoids premise thinking. It is, itself, rebellious.

The play *State of Siege* is an echo of *The Plague*. The play is heavy-handed and lacking in subtlety. Men, not a disease, are the adversaries in *State of Siege*, with one called The Plague and one called Nada. All oppressive forces in *State of Siege* are of human origin. The tyrannical, dictatorial, and totalitarian governments of the world are symbolized in the character called The Plague, his henchmen, the Law, and the church. Diego and Victoria, the principal characters, rebel against the impositions of The Plague and his regime.

In *State of Siege* the judge (Victoria's father) and the priest refuse or fail to act for the people, but cooperate instead with the oppressors. The Plague and his cohorts, unlike the pestilence in *The Plague*, are a social force, springing from the midst of the people. Inhabitants of the beleaguered city reveal their character as they relate to The Plague.

Though he is finally heroic, Diego, the principal male character in the play, is initially as fully focused on achieving happiness as was Rambert in the novel. He, like Rieux, is drawn to medicine as vocation. Like Tarrou, he recognizes that there is an undesirable quality in him which can be transmitted to others. He fears infecting them.

In his first encounters with The Plague, Diego is primarily concerned for his own safety. Victoria, his fiancee, is appalled by what she regards as his cowardly acts. Challenged, inspired and motivated by Victoria's love and her courage, Diego changes. He becomes a heroic rebel. In his changed state he incarnates the exemplary traits of the man in revolt.

The Plague's creation of suffering and his assault on happiness, Victoria's inspiration, and Diego's belief in the basic innocence of humans combine to firm Diego for rebellion. Diego's acts of rebellion launch the movement which causes The Plague and his agents to relent and finally retire from the city. But the rebellion costs Diego his life. He dies to save Victoria and the terrorized city.

The play strongly asserts that oppressive regimes are best met, not by collaboration, but by resistance. In standing up to The Plague, Diego inspires others to join the revolt, leading to the final extraction of the city from The Plague's reign. The people's resistance causes the wind of freedom to blow in from the sea.

Diego, like Rambert in *The Plague*, held happiness as his primary goal. Both ascended from self-concern to great consideration for others, under the inspiration of another person. Diego finally faced up to The Plague because of the abuse and the destruction of human happiness.

The goal of happiness—that at-home-ness in the universe to which humans are entitled—was Diego's nostalgia. When challenged by Victoria he came to understand fully that human happiness was besieged by the political tyranny of rulers-by-force. So he confronted *The Plague*. He stood up for the citizens of Cadiz, daring the ruler on his own turf, causing him to slink away before the rising winds of freedom from the sea. Diego, late in the play, is an exemplar of the rebel who is fully described, later, in *The Rebel*.

State of Siege is a flawed play. Symbolism is flagrantly obvious, and the mixture of dramatic forms does not enhance character delineation. As a consequence, the characters are not full-formed, and characters change without believable motivation. Diego, the protagonist, moves suddenly from selfish concern to the admirable selflessness of giving up his life, the great change coming without substantial motivation. Likewise, The Plague also changes precipitately, is no longer the virulent threat he once was. Thus, the denouement is romantic hyperbole.

State of Siege departs from Camus's established mode. It is unambiguous advocacy of a course of action. The intent is commendable, and its message is clear: tyranny is defeated by direct confrontation. But this unambiguous message did not make for a good play, nor did it contribute to the play's effectiveness as a vehicle for consideration of rebellion.

From the perspective of the absurd—or lucidity, the continuing portion of the absurd—the play falls short. *The Myth of Sisyphus* set forth nostalgia and the irrational as the two foci necessary for observing and understanding the world. There is the irrational and human response to it—the search for meaning in life in face of the irrational. But, regardless of the potency of nostalgia—or its absence among those who have given up the search for meaning—the irrational continues. Philosophies, ideologies, theologies motivated by nostalgia may be discredited, fall, or be cast away, but the irrational persists, either in the absurd or in lucidity, its refined form.

In *State of Siege*, however, Diego's belated but heroic revolt defeats and destroys The Plague, symbol of the irrational. The import of the play, then, is that human opposition and resistance may defeat and obliterate the irrational. If that is the case, the tension between the irrational and nostalgia need no longer—can no longer—be maintained. The impetus for revolt is no more, for the irrational has been definitively defeated, though at the price of the revolt's leader. The play displays a strong instance of triumphant nostalgia and thus constitutes a soteriological allegory.

In defense of Camus, it may be said that he was exercising his normal, characteristic form of thought, that is, rebellious thought, and that he has simply rebelled against the thought with which he began. But revolt, the basis of rebellious thinking, rises from the coexistence of nostalgia and the irrational. If there is no irrational, revolt or rebellion is no longer imperative.

The play—almost more pageant than play—was not well received. Camus noted that "there was no dissenting voice among the critics," and they gave it "a unanimous slashing" when it opened in Paris. "Yet," he said, "with all its shortcomings, it is, of all my writings, the one that most resembles me." It is not a traditional play, he said, but a work intended "to mix all the dramatic forms of expression, from the lyric monologue to collective theatre, including pantomime, simple dialogue, farce, and the dramatic chorus."

From this we surmise that Camus's theatrical preferences—and perhaps his artistic concerns—dominated in this instance, and overcame his characteristic mode of rebellious thought.

Paradoxically, the failure of *State of Siege* substantiates one of Camus's dicta. He objected to the "thesis work"—one which begins with and supports a thesis. *State of Siege* is such a work. Camus's delineation of it as "of all my writings, the one that most resembles me," is simply inexplicable. The play was not consonant with his usual mode of rebellious thought. It did not serve Camus well. Nevertheless, in the final outcome, Diego, who loses his life in standing up for others, does model some of the qualities of a rebel for others.

The several types of rebels, near-rebels, and counter-rebels presented in *The Misunderstanding*, *The Plague*, and *State of Siege* provided for the distillation of the true rebel's essential attributes. Grand, Rambert, Tarrou, and Diego foreshadow Dora Dulebov and Ivan Kaliayev of *The Just Assassins*, a play. Based on incidents in the lives of these historical characters, the play shows rebels at the zenith of admirability.

V

Portrait of Rebellion

Camus does not harmonize his later thought with his previous articulations, showing little concern for order and system. *The Myth of Sisyphus* presents absurd thought and the absurd stance, with the consequences of freedom, quantity (or passion), and revolt. All coincide with happiness: "Happiness and the absurd are two sons of the same earth. They are inseparable," he said in *The Myth*. Yet, as we have seen, the lives of his fictional characters did not present such happiness. He did not intend to make a logical demonstration of the proof of a proposition.

Nostalgia and the irrational survive the demise of Camus's absurd. But the consequences of the absurd are compromised, at the very least, in his fiction: The consequence of freedom is de-absolutized—it is no longer unlimited. Quantity as a basic feature is discredited by its excesses. Revolt alone continues as a strong remnant. And revolt, modified into rebellion in *The Rebel*, is elevated to the position of ascendancy previously held by the absurd stance.

None of this setting aside is specifically detailed by Camus. Looking back to make "corrections" is apparently of no concern. Revision or rescission is eschewed, if not disdained. His thought progresses and moves away from previous declarations or avowals, without indication or admission that any shift is being made. His approach is not systematic. He does not create a seamless fabric. He presents neither a coherent order nor a congruent philosophy directly.

Revolt, central to *The Rebel*, is depicted as one of several consequences of the absurd stance in *The Myth*. The absurd is felt by humans who yearn to know but are confronted by a universe which is enigmatic, beyond the grasping of the human mind. Human rationality faces the irrationality of the universe. The absurd person, becoming conscious of the stand-off, brings it into full awareness, and takes on the absurd stance: admission and maintenance of the confrontation between the irrationality of the universe and the human yearning for meaning in it.

The absurd is basically cosmic, with the universe as the arena. Most humans shrink the dimensions and dwell contentedly within systems of thought—philosophical, theological, or ideological, whether banal or sophisticated—which impose some order on the disorder of the irrational. Those who accept some version of order have committed philosophical suicide. But the absurd human refuses all explication, believing that the cosmos does not yield to the ordering of the human mind. Those taking the absurd stance refuse to grant the universe an order which it doesn't have. They are strangers to the bulk, the great mass, of humanity.

In *The Rebel* Camus turns from the absurd human to the rebel. Two focuses are possible. One is revolt against the state of things: that quarrel is with the gods. The other is rebellion against the human order which oppresses: that quarrel is with humans. Rebels become conscious of a condition to which they object. Perceiving that the condition is imposed upon them, they confront and oppose those who have inflicted it.

The rebels' "no"—most often against human imposition—implies a universal value. The "no" springs from a felt intrusion on that value. It intimates the infraction of a basic rule of life. Human nature has been insulted, according to the rebel. Rebellion contributes to a deeper knowledge of that nature which has not yet been fully discovered. The rebel, even though rebellion may more directly defy men than gods, has cosmic concerns. By defying human imposers the rebel affirms humankind and defines a portion of human nature.

By the act of rebellion, often at the risk of life, rebels elevate the common good above their own good. Though asserting self, that assertion, since the rebels risk their own well-being, is on behalf of others. They stand up for something which does not belong to them alone. They affirm a value basic to humanity. This is substantive enough for Camus to proclaim, for the rebel, "I rebel, therefore we exist."

Rebellion, of course, is always an act of opposition to someone or something. When humans revolt against the universal condition of humanity, there is metaphysical rebellion. When rebel slaves set themselves against the master or the order/system which oppresses, there is social rebellion. The two types, the metaphysical and the social, are linked in Camus's thought with the phenomenon of Christianity.

The idea of a personal God, who is responsible for everything since he created everything, gives meaning to human protest. Camus understands that the Christ addressed the problems of death and evil. And those are precisely the problems which sting the mind of the rebel. Golgotha, where the man-god suffered and despaired, is important in human history because there divinity experienced the agony of death. But when humans, with Reason, challenged the notion of Christ's divinity, the way was prepared for humans to rebel against their state and status in the universe.

Camus sees Dostoevsky's Ivan Karamazov as the representative man who questions God's morality. Ivan proclaims mankind's innocence and asserts that death is an unjust sentence, a punishment without cause. For Camus, Ivan is the incarnation of the refusal of salvation, a refusal based on the ground of God's injustice. Yet Ivan perceives that the rebellion against God, the one who visits death on humans, leaves humans with a dilemma. If God's rule is denied, then everything is permitted and humans are free to establish a rule over life, including the control of death. Acting on this belief, Ivan permits his own father to be killed.

The major purpose of *The Rebel* is to warn humanity against turning rebellion into revolution. Ivan's metaphysical rebellion—his defiance of God because of God's injustice—evolves into metaphysical revolution. The master of the world has been set aside and humans are now free to establish a human order. God's order is replaced with the order of humans. But Ivan's turning from rebellion to revolution has the most severe consequences. It leads to his madness. In thus linking revolution, madness, and death Camus is strongly warning against the delusion of revolution.

Camus says that Friedrich Nietzsche brought the absence of eternal values out into the open. Since God is dead, at least in the hearts of humans, there are no operative eternal values. Nihilism, a product of rebellion, is brought to consciousness. Humans, in God's absence, become responsible for everything and must discover or create their own law and order. Attainment of the kingdom of heaven is left to the achievement of humans.

Furthermore, by denying God, the rebel can now aspire to replace him. The divinity of humans thus becomes conceivable. In Nietzsche's terms, the salvation of mankind is not to be achieved in heaven by God, but on earth by humans. Thus surfaces the doctrine of super humanity. With this theory Nietzsche replaces the Beyond of Christianity with the Later On of mankind. And so is opened the way for the reign of Reason and of History.

Having discussed the contributions of Dostoevsky and Nietzsche, Camus turns to historical rebellion. He sums up his philosophical considerations of the origins of rebellion by asserting that the rebel is really asking for reasons for living. The rebel's fight against death is a way of claiming that there is meaning in life, a way of striving for order and unity. Camus says that the rebel, though without conscious knowledge of the fact, is searching for a moral philosophy or a religion. In rebelling against divinity humans build the universe into a strongpoint from which to further assault the deposed deity. The metaphysical rebels attacked the heavens and drove God out, then turned to the use of Reason as a weapon, a singularly human means of conquest available to them.

Then, in order to demonstrate the motivation of rebellion and its tendency to evolve into revolution, Camus recalls Spartacus's rebellion. Spartacus and seventy other gladiators rose against their Roman masters, demanding "equal rights" for slaves. The rebellion soon gathered up a force of seventy thousand insurgents who freed the slaves and made them masters over their former masters. The rebels replaced the deposed order with their own, continuing the institution of slavery—the very system which had provoked their own rebellion.

Rebellion turned into revolution and almost succeeded in supplanting the power of Rome itself. Spartacus's troops turned back only when they finally faced the citadel of Rome, as if awed by the sacred walls, the city of the gods. There the spirit of rebellion faltered before the intimidating symbol, the divinely supported city. But later on, Camus points out, rebels, inspired in part by Christianity itself, dared to assail nobles and kings, those who were seen as the earthly representatives of God.

This assailing took place in Christian France, when the religion of Reason was instituted in the French Revolution. Reason replaced Christianity as a faith. The nation became a Republic, one of law and order, with the will of the people substituted for the will of God. Reason sat on the throne of God, and the King, as representative of the divine prerogative, was pulled down. Louis XVI was executed.

Camus refers to the death of Louis as a Passion, symbolizing the secularization of Western history, as the disembodiment of the Christian God. The doctrine of this religion of Reason held that a few must die in order that the great number might be saved. For Camus this revolution signaled the beginning of the reign of History. The Historical Imperative demands the subservience of the many to the few who know the direction in which History is moving.

History may be imperialistic—and Camus identifies many courtiers of that empire—but history per se reveals the long opposition of master and slave. The master provokes the slave's consciousness of his servility. History records the results of the extended efforts of slaves to secure their real freedom.

The context of history provides the setting for the evolution of mankind's divinity, with the tacit, if not the open, admission that divinity can be achieved only at the end of time. Thus, within a history without God, the future provides the only transcendence. But there are those in history who passionately deny the tyranny of the future, as well as the prerogative of the master, and affirm the equal value of all human lives. The Russian, Ivan Kaliayev, defied these tyrannies. For Camus, Kaliayev was the purest of rebels.

Of all the "men of 1905," says Camus, Kaliayev knew and practiced compassion for others. Out of concern for the Russian masses under the reign of the Czars, Kaliayev went to the extreme of killing to bring down tyranny. But, in payment for the taking of another life, he accepted his own death by execution. By this self-sacrifice Kaliayev affirmed a value that surpassed himself. For Camus, Ivan Kaliayev and Dora Brilliant, a fellow revolutionary, represented the highest reaches of rebellious consciousness. They were the inspiration for *The Just Assassins*, one of Camus's stage plays.

After the achievements of the people of 1905, rebellion suffered decline into revolution, as had other rebellions before it. Camus held these transmutations to be so objectionable and dangerous that he wrote *The Rebel* in opposition.

For Camus, the State is at best a necessary evil. Humankind needs some kind of order to prevent the strong from tyrannizing the weak. But the power of the State is such that leaders can use it for their own ends, to the detriment of the bulk of humanity. Unfortunately, reinforcement of the power of the State has been the result of all modern revolutions, according to Camus. The State as master thus often creates revolt and rebellion. (Strangely, Camus does not discuss the American Revolution, perhaps because he saw little change or essential difference between the British and the American forms of government.)

Camus aligns himself with rebellion as distinct from revolution. For revolution acts to impose its values on all people. Rebellion, however, is faithful to the principle of the solidarity of all humankind. Moreover, in its emergence it defines a value for humanity.

From this perspective *The Rebel* presents analyses of the revolutions of Nazi Socialism and Russian Communism. In his analysis Camus paid far more attention to the Russian than to the German example, perhaps because the Nazi revolution was terminated, whereas the Marxist revolution continued in Camus's own time.

The revolution in Germany was an embracing of the irrational. Since there is no universal order, the leaders decided, humans are entitled or permitted to impose their own. So the Nazis under Hitler concocted a set of values drawn from the philosophy of the gang, translated it into an ideal of superhumanity, and sought to force the two upon a whole civilization. The values of the few were pressed down upon the many. Most of the many in Germany accepted these values as profitable for themselves—and the world remembers the consequences of that criminal aggrandizement.

Germany took the concept of freedom to its ultimate manifestation, recognizing no limits, defying all values except its own self-serving set. Ruthless values inaugurated a revolution and strongly increased the power of the state over its people. The effect was the emboldening of Hitler to attempt the forced impression of his values on the whole world. Nazi Socialism represented the ascendancy of the irrational and the glorification of freedom.

Unlike the Nazis, Russian Communism opted for nostalgia, instead of the irrational. Proclaiming above all the value of justice, it imposed its own order, in the face of an orderless universe. Then, contrary to the perspective of Karl Marx, with whom Camus agreed, the Russians assumed the legitimacy of almost every type of means in order to move toward the goal of a just and classless society. Marx had said, "An end that requires unjust means is not a just end." But the Russians, concentrating on the future, justified the suppression of contemporary humans in order to provide, they said, for the ideal of a classless society sometime in the future.

Camus's basic charge against the Russian revolution is that the promise of justice in the distant future was used to justify pervasive injustice in the present. The totalitarian regime, with the laudable goal of a society where all are equal, imposed near-total bondage on the people. Everything was justified by the promise of a future miracle: the transformation of the imposed order into a universal republic of free leisure! All this was based on a faulty premise: The crushing of freedom will create, some day, an empire of freedom.

In the objectification of the individual—a consequence deriving from the basic theory of the communist ideal—Camus discovered the grounds for rebellion: Humans naturally resent their classification as objects. Some refuse to be used as objects, as pawns for the benefit of a long-distant Maybe. Some resist even to the point of self-extinction, to their own deaths. By that dying, Camus asserts, people affirm the value of human nature as something bigger than they are, something beyond them, a kind of transcendence. With these rebels, Camus believes that to love humans is to love them in the present, and that any regime which loves only those who have not yet appeared must be resisted.

The heart of *The Rebel* is found in Camus's distinction between rebellion and revolution. Perceived wrongs trigger rebellion: a slave rebels against his master; a people revolts against its oppressors. The rebel acts to bring about the rectification of wrongs, to force change. He acts to make the order more humane, more responsive to the needs of himself and other human beings. Humanity, the rebel says, in language resonating with that of religion, must be reborn or it will die. The renaissance must be depended upon.

Rebels, whether tacitly or consciously, recognize the reality of human nature—all humans are sisters and brothers. This recognition keeps rebels from assuming the role of master. It prevents them from using others as objects to be manipulated for their own ends. It manifests the understanding that all humans are equal in value, though their talents may vary widely.

But the most profound characteristic of the true rebels may be lucidity. They know the vast irrationality of the universe. They admit that the yearning for order may tempt them to impose their order on others. They are aware of the need for constant rebellion and recognize that, were their order instituted, a continuous revolt would be required to keep it humane. Therefore, they do not seek to establish their order as normative for all, or even a portion, of humankind. They follow rebellious thought in eschewing the progression from assumption to premise to conclusion to imposition. Theirs is rebellious deportment.

Revolution, in contrast to rebellion, does impose itself. It begins in rebellion against an unjust order. Then, dropping its character of rebellion, it supplants the order against which it had rebelled. To protect itself, to establish its own validity, to affirm its own values, the revolution assumes the features of that order which it had despised. It becomes the new order, an order which invariably spawns revolt and rebellion.

The slave has rebelled and become the master. As master he creates slaves who are provoked into rebellion. The rebel-become-revolutionary cannot avoid the inevitable: imposed order is rebelled against; rebellion organizes and supplants the domineering order; the new order is rebelled against . . . and so on, ad infinitum.

In *The Myth* Camus objected to the thesis novel, the novel "beginning with a smug thought" which it then sets out to manifest and establish. With validity of the thesis assumed, support is assembled to prove that validity. . . . So it is with revolution: it believes that it is right and good for humanity; it consolidates its position; it arms itself for defense against those who question its rightness.

The succession from rebellion to revolution can be avoided, Camus asserts, by recognizing and honoring the need for constant revision of any order. He who forgets his rebellious origins necessarily becomes a policeman and an administrator who turns against rebellion. When he forgets his origins in rebellion the revolutionary operates on the premise that he can remold humanity so that it will accept his order. The revolutionary without memory fails to recognize that all humans are basically rebels—the scheme of things has taught them to be—until or unless they have been subdued and enslaved. The revolutionary who is not simultaneously a rebel, that is, one who expresses and practices openness to the constant revision of accepted order, is not a true revolutionary.

Rebels, when true to character, insist upon limits. They apply these limits to their own conclusions, constantly striving to improve the sketches which they draw in the effort to re-create some part of the universe's wild disorder. They use pencil, avoiding the permanence of ink, for they know that humans can never overcome the vast irrationality of the universe, though the attempt to do so must be continuously made.

Rebellion is at odds with History when History is defined as the inevitable, that great Later On in behalf of which humans are to sacrifice and be sacrificed. Those who make demands on humans for the sake of History are to be rebelliously resisted. Rebellion passionately defies those imperatives which decree killing and dying for the molding of humans into something which they are not. Rebellion vigorously contends for the living and the letting-live which will take humans toward the creative fulfillment of what they already are.

Part IV of *The Rebel* features rebellious thought in discussing rebellion and the novel. Camus sees the novel as a correction, a reformulation of the world in which we live. It is a creation which may reflect mankind's deepest wishes regarding the world of our existence. Employing language as a tool, the novelist distributes realistic elements drawn from life into the unity and shape of the artistic universe which is created.

Artistic creation in the hands of the rebel seeks to impress its laws on the world. Some artistic geniuses have succeeded in this, says Camus, as he repeats Shelley's observation that "poets are the unacknowledged legislators of the world." These acts of creation, by their very existence, deny the world of tyrants and slaves. That miserable world which we endure can only be brought to death and transfiguration by rebellious acts of creation. In fact, every political reformer, Camus believes, tries to create in reality what Shakespeare, Moliere, Cervantes, and Tolstoy set forth—a world perennially ready to fulfill the yearning for real human freedom and dignity which every person deeply feels at heart.

Turning to violence and murder—which rebellion implies—Camus speaks to both. His words provide a striking repudiation of the belief that the good of the many justifies the sacrifice of the few who stand in the way of that good. If there is no higher meaning beyond humans, if one human is only accountable to another, then one automatically excludes oneself from the world when he violently removes another human being from it. If rebels allow themselves to commit murder they can reconcile themselves with that extreme act in only one way: by accepting their own sacrifice and death. In that killing and self-dying they show that murder is impossible, elevating the "We are" above the "We will be." Adherence to this high ideal accounts for the calm happiness and serenity of two who killed and died. Both Kaliayev and Saint Just tranquilly accepted death on the scaffold and the guillotine.

As if speaking directly to Meursault and Caligula, Camus declares in *The Rebel* that the freedom to kill, the most extreme form of freedom, is not compatible with rebellion. Rebellion does not itself demand total freedom. Quite to the contrary, it puts freedom on trial. The rebel insists that the presence of another human being restricts the exercise of freedom. That limitation comes from the individual's power to rebel, a power the rebel knows well. That freedom which the rebel claims is claimed for everybody. The freedom denied by the rebel is denied everybody, as well.

Rebels are rebels, says Camus, because they are surrounded by falsehood, injustice, and violence. They are, however, in a veritable dilemma. For in resisting these conditions, they cannot unequivocally swear never to lie or to kill—to do so would be to denounce their rebellion, to accept evil and murder. Neither can they agree to kill and to lie for that would be to justify murder and violence, to destroy the very reasons for the insurrection. Rebels, therefore, can never find peace. They know what is good, but to effect it they may have to do evil. But if they are finally driven to kill, they will themselves accept death. So Kaliayev, climbing to the hangman's noose, defines the limits, the exact limits, which show where a human's honor begins and ends.

Camus's most telling observation about the relationship between rebellion and revolution comes in his statement that revolution sets the stage for the commencement of another rebellion. Revolution seeks to conserve the energy expended, to justify the battle, by proving and establishing itself. Then it is compelled to deny the rebellion which inevitably arises in opposition to the revolution's establishment. When rebellion loses its way, its identity, and turns into revolution, it is no longer to be called rebellion. There is, then, an inextinguishable opposition between the movement, the action, and the dynamism of rebellion and the fortified establishment of revolution.

A philosophy of rebellion, says Camus, if it is possible for rebellion to have a philosophy, would emphasize limits, the recognition of ignorance, and the risk of opposition. Basic to rebellion is the admission by rebels that they do not know everything, and hence, that they cannot kill everyone or order everything to fit in with their perception of the proper order. The honoring of limits is the essence of rebellion.

Two major ideals are involved in rebellion: justice and freedom. The rebels' sense of justice is outraged, and freedom propels them to resistance. Total justice denies freedom. Absolute freedom mocks justice. In the tension between freedom and justice the limits of each are found. This counter-action is similar to that between nostalgia and the irrational, as Camus presented them in *The Myth*. These two held in tension produce lucidity, that great good emanating from his analysis of the absurd. Here in *The Rebel* rebellious thought brings in the strength of freedom to counter the force of justice (which was barely touched upon in the discussion of the absurd). So freedom in tension with justice yields rebellion. The hyphen mark symbolizes rebellious thought: The couplings of nostalgia-irrational and freedom-justice define, correct, and limit. The opposition of forces is the great generic principle on which Camus's rebellious thought depends.

Violence is not denied as a rebellious means. But violence is a last resort. True and authentic rebels will employ arms only for the defense of institutions which limit violence. They refuse to defend those who adopt violence as a means for building and buttressing their own order. Thus, limits are lifted up as the essence of rebellion. These are consciously adopted limits, not those imposed by circumstances. When rebellion forgets this and permits itself to be limited only by expediency, it allows limitless enslavement.

The revolutionary mind must remain faithful to rebellious origins, must be committed to the thought that recognizes limits. Rebellion issues from the recognition of the commonality of human nature. This leads rebels to realize, unlike absurd persons, that they are not alone. Acknowledging the existence of others like themselves produces the very limitation which arises when humans honor themselves by the consciousness of each other.

Some thinkers argue that Camus's type of rebellion is too tame. But he argues that, since rebellion without restraint readily becomes-revolution-becomes-imposed order-becomes-cause for rebellion, the better course is for rebels to delimit their rebellion. Others may believe that they will install a perfected order, but rebels understand that perfection is not achievable. It is better to engage in moderate rebellion, in order to prevent one more metamorphosis from rebellion to tyranny. So rebellion and moderation are to be linked. Rebellion requires moderation, defends moderation, re-creates moderation in history. Concomitantly, moderation can only continue through the exercise of rebellion. Conflict continually created, continuously resolved, is the outcome of rebellion. Perpetual conflict may thus be created, but that conflict may be kept within the limits of moderation.

Camus sums up his treatise on rebellion by asserting that "Rebellion cannot exist without a strange form of love. Those who find no rest in God or in history are condemned to live for those who, like themselves, cannot live: in fact, for the humiliated. . . . Real generosity toward the future lies in giving all to the present. Rebellion proves . . . that it is the very movement of life and that it cannot be denied without renouncing life."

In conclusion Camus recalls Karamazov's saying that if all are not saved the salvation of one only is not a great good. Camus adds: "The rebel rejects divinity in order to share in the struggles and destiny of all men. . . . All may indeed live again, side by side with the martyrs of 1905, but only on condition that it is understood that they correct one another and that a limit under the sun shall curb them all. Each tells the other that he is not God. This is the end of romanticism."

Rebellion knows that it must risk culpability, though it seeks innocence, its opposite. When drawn together, these opposites moderate each other. They are merged into the concept and the person of the innocent murderer. For exemplar Camus advances Kaliayev in *The Just Assassins*.

A dramatization of the principal theme of *The Rebel*, the play comes very close to being the "thesis work" which Camus objected to. In the preface to the book of plays containing *The Just*, (*Caligula and Three Other Plays*, Vintage, New York, 1958) he says that he tried to employ the classical means of opposition between characters of equal strength and reason. But, equal or not, Camus's sympathies are clearly with Kaliayev and Dora. He says as much in the preface: "My admiration for my heroes, Kaliayev and Dora, is complete. I merely wanted to show that action itself had limits." Yet the antagonist, Stepan, is given respectability and considerable strength of character of his own. Camus provides for change and development in him, making him much more sympathetic at the end. Nevertheless, the interaction of the principal characters, Kaliayev and Stepan, clearly reveals the author's deep attachment to Kaliayev. In that sense the play comes close to being the thesis work which he decried— for the play sets out and supports a point of view. Kaliayev is a representation of Camus's ideal rebel, a rebel passionately devoted to limits.

In various ways the reader learns that Kaliayev is a poet, a lover of life, one given to laughter and gaiety. He's in love with beauty and happiness. He dreams of the day when all men are brothers. In contrast, Stepan says that he hates his fellowman, that he loves not life, but justice. Stepan cries out that he would strike at the masses themselves in order to rescue humanity from itself and from bondage. Kaliayev responds that Stepan loves only the man of the future while he, Kaliayev, strives to serve the man of the present.

The two characters represent contrary commitments. One is a commitment to history and the Later On. The other attends above all to the present and the people of the present. Stepan's avowal of willingness to save the masses of the future by striking down those of the present appears to Kaliayev to present the threat of another despotism as despicable as that which both he and Stepan are resisting.

Dora provides the way to gauge the characters of the two men. She is at first most like Stepan. She's devoted to the cause, a lover of justice, in firm control of her emotions. Yet she particularly likes Borea Annenkov, another character, because his heart is not dried up. She is sensitive to the Grand Duke's humanity, even though he is the object of their bombing attempt. But her heart is set on a present justice. And she gladly admits that those whose hearts are set on justice have no right to love, thus revealing the reason for hiding her feelings.

All the principal characters are involved in violence. Stepan, flogged unmercifully when in prison, dwells on that experience, and is opposed to violence. But he is willing to join in the bomb plot. While still voicing his opposition to violence, Kaliayev is chosen by the other rebels to throw the bomb at the Grand Duke and he accepts the assignment. He proclaims that the group is forced to violence, compelled to be murderers. He claims that in killing the Grand Duke he will be killing not a man but the specter of despotism.

After the bombing, which he carries out after a failed first attempt, Kaliayev is called upon to speak with the Grand Duchess, widow of the assassinated Grand Duke. He insists that he threw the bomb at tyranny and not at a man, asserting that he only carried out a just verdict. Then, later, just before his execution for the assassination, he speaks his last words in "protesting with all the manhood in me against violence."

A vehement interchange between Stepan and Kaliayev brings out their major differences. The quarrel occurs when Kaliayev returns to their flat after his failure to throw the bomb the first time. Kaliayev had seen the Grand Duke's children in the carriage with him, and hesitated so long that it was too late to throw. After days of planning and hours of danger the group was jeopardized by this non-action. In his tearful confession of failure Kaliayev recalled his great fear, at home in the Ukraine, of running down children with his horses.

Stepan accuses Kaliayev of squeamishness and rank disobedience in refusing to throw the bomb. Balking at the killing of children is a strange weakness, Stepan shouts, which condemns thousands of Russian children to death. But Kaliayev protests vigorously that killing children would be a crime against a man's honor. Dora stands with Kaliayev. She supports his decision not to kill the children, crying out that the killing of children would bring the loathing of humanity upon the movement. But Stepan protests that the revolution is being betrayed because of the fastidiousness of Kaliayev. He objects to the "sentimentalizing" about children. In the end, however, the group decides that Kaliayev is right, that violence must have limits.

The matter of limits is the large difference between the two positions. Stepan says there are no limits to acts for bringing about the reformed society which must be the Russia of the future. But Dora and Kaliayev argue that there are limits and that the killing of children goes beyond the limits, thus affirming the Camusian ideal of limits.

The ideal of limits, however, is not confined to the question of killing children. Murder for the cause must be limited in other ways—as Kaliayev shows in his submission to execution. For Kaliayev, murder entails—indeed, requires—the murderer's death also. To commit murder is also to accept one's own death. In truth, Kaliayev dies for his ideal, believing that to be the only way to prove oneself worthy of that ideal. He and Stepan share a goal—that of justice for the people of Russia—but they differ in that Stepan would kill repeatedly for justice whereas Kaliayev would kill but once. Forced into being a murderer, he can be innocent of it by dying himself. He takes the Grand Duke's life with the full intention of giving up his own as well, so that murder may not triumph over life, for murder is a crime against humanity itself.

At one point Kaliayev, who loves life, speaks of the loathsome world in which he lives. It is loathsome to this lover of humanity because of repression and murder within it. To survive after killing the Grand Duke would be to accept this loathsomeness, but by dying he would both keep the agreement he made with his brothers and show that murder is not allowable.

The interview with the Grand Duchess, in Kaliayev's cell after the bombing, shows the strange truth of Kaliayev. He shows revulsion at the accusation of murder yet he is certain he acted justly in committing it. Kaliayev is thoroughly repelled by the Grand Duchess's description of her husband's bloody corpse. He cries out that he is no murderer. He forbids her asking pardon of man or of God for his act, insisting that he had not killed a man. Yet, after his almost hysterical denial, he goes to the gallows quietly, giving his life for the one he's taken.

Dora supports Kaliayev in all that he does. She tells her comrades, as they wait for news about Kaliayev in prison, "It's our duty to wish that he may die." Then, finally, in words resonant with Camus himself, she exults, after Kaliayev's execution. "Don't you realize this is the day of our justification . . . a sign for all the revolutionaries of the world. Yanek [Kaliayev] is a murderer no longer." The ideal of innocent murderer had been fulfilled in Ivan Kaliayev.

The Just Assassins dramatizes *The Rebel* as *The Stranger* dramatized *The Myth of Sisyphus*. Kaliayev presented himself to the gallows in recognition of the impossibility of murder: in demonstration of his solidarity with his fellowman, the Grand Duke; and in delineation of rebellion's limits. Meursault, the absurd man, killed without cause of hatred, anger, or principle. He killed because to pull the trigger or not amounted to the same thing. He felt no remorse, as if his victim were not a man, and knew himself a stranger to the majority of humans. His condemnation to death he saw as one more absurdity. He coveted cries of execration for his last moments—for he was solitary, alone in the universe. Meursault wins our sympathy, for he was mishandled by circumstance; but Kaliayev wins our admiration, for he created the circumstances for his own martyrdom.

From the acts of Dora Brilliant (Dulebov in the play) and Ivan Kaliayev Camus has drawn a portrait of rebellious limits. Kaliayev enacted the extremity of limits in yielding up his life because he'd taken the life of another. No matter that the life was taken to better the chances for justice, no matter that the cause was praiseworthy—Kaliayev showed that murder is undertaken at extreme cost. Death limits death. Surely the world would see infinitely less bloodshed if those with power to kill were to honor rebellion's limits.

VI

Gentle Vision and Vehement Irony

Camus felt driven to write *The Rebel*, though he knew it would trigger antagonism and controversy. In fact, its publication led to the final split with long-time friend Jean-Paul Sartre. The two men characteristically responded differently to issues they both faced. Sartre was revolutionary, Camus rebellious in outlook. *The Rebel* forcefully set forth the rebel stance as infinitely preferable to the revolutionary. The slowly opening fissure which had been growing between the two men now became a chasm. Across the void they resisted each other, their altercation carried on through several issues of literary journals, with Sartre calling in reinforcements to put Camus down. Camus felt pummelled and abused through the controversy. He turned to other subjects. He moved back, in part, to quiet themes similar to those in *L'Envers et L'Endroit*. He tried new techniques or extensions of older ones.

Exile and the Kingdom, a collection of stories, includes some which Camus referred to as exercises in "realistic writing." But these are not simply descriptive pieces. Some exert a lingering percolative effect in the parabolic manner. They continue to brew in the subconscious, rising and then flooding through the mind long after the tale has been told. Interpretation of them must be partially tentative, for there is a stirring element in them which may elicit new insight after some delay. There is strength in even the gentlest force exerted by Camus.

In the collection, for the most part, Camus presents a gentle vision. Though the conscious ambiguity of earlier fiction is not absent, it is reduced. Some of the stories are positively straightforward depictions of life, without either mystery or definite import. Some are softly parabolic, without the driving force of *Caligula* or *The Just Assassins*.

Exile and the Kingdom is not unconnected with elements from Camus's past. Autobiographical elements reverberate in passages speaking of exile in the midst of others, and of lonely striving to achieve a distant goal. Attitudinal sets of which Camus strongly disapproved are often subverted by implication in some of the material.

"The Silent Men" may be called "realistic writing." It reflects something of Camus's youth—his uncle was a cooper in Algiers, and the boy Camus appears in a photo of the work force. The woody, smoky smells of the shop, the clutter of wood, the sounds of saw, chisel and plane, the banging of the riveting hammer all reveal a real place. The story set there tells of an unusual day in the last days of a dying industry.

The coopers are under threat of displacement by fabricators of metal containers. The coopers' wooden casks are more costly and less durable than the newer products. Yvars, the protagonist, and his fellow coopers had unwisely gone on strike for better pay, the cost of living having risen faster than their wages. The strikers, gaining only half-hearted support from the general union, decide to return to work after several weeks without pay. Their return is a tacit admission that they were wrong and that Lassalle, the owner, was right.

Relations between employer and employees are naturally strained upon the strikers' return. Lassalle, who has been a generous boss, with real affection for his workmen, attempts to re-establish cordial relations, but is rebuffed. He is irritated by the coopers' complete lack of response. Yvars regrets the continuing breach, but can do nothing about it.

With quiet understatement Camus describes the brief meeting when Yvars and Ballester, the shop foreman, are called in to the boss's home for a talk. Lassalle tries once more to re-establish friendly relations, but the men find it impossible to reply in kind. Still silent, the two return to their unaccustomed work and find some satisfaction in the resumption of almost-abandoned skills.

During their brief time in the boss's home they hear that his little girl is sick and put to bed with the hope that she'll recover. After lunch, however, the foreman is told to bring in a doctor. Soon after the doctor's visit, an ambulance arrives to take the child to the hospital, her illness serious but still undiagnosed. Though the men of the shop are sympathetic, they make no attempt to express their compassion to the family.

Yvars returns to his home that night, tired from the day's work and saddened by the distress of the boss's family. He tells his wife that he regrets his inability to communicate his true feelings. He wonders if they should go somewhere else and start over.... So the story ends.

Is the story anything more than a realistic portrayal of strained relations between owners and laborers? Clearly, economic facts have put a barrier between Lassalle and the men. The fellow-feeling elicited by the little girl's illness is not sufficient to overcome that barrier. Men, here naturally sympathetic, are constrained by economics. Marxist theorists might be pleased with this import of the story, but Camus had resolutely detached himself from Marxist positions.

The "more" of the story may be found in Yvars's gimpy leg and the title of the collection. The story centers on Yvars. Yvars is disabled, pedalling himself to work and back on a bicycle with one rigid, non-working pedal. So he is particularly touched by the threat of the little girl's illness. But Yvars couldn't show sympathy with the man—or the system—which had crippled him economically. So, though suffering bound Yvars and Lassalle together, social position and economics kept them apart. The basic solidarity of men—which Yvars felt—was fractured by economic circumstances. He considers going away. . . . Though it is not said, we may infer that he feels exiled, that this is not the kingdom. He thinks of going away . . . in search of the kingdom.

"The Artist at Work," in *Exile and the Kingdom*, also appears as a mimodrame in Gallimard's Pleiade edition of Camus's works. Both pieces are hyperbolized depictions of the artist's predicament in society, with autobiographical connections.

In the story Jonas's success as a painter comes without great effort on his part—as some claimed of Camus. Jonas is propelled into applying his genius. Family, friends, and wife push him, then hedge him in by friendly acts which smother him. His artistic capacity is choked off. Family demands detract him. Admiring friends inundate him with compliments and advice, keep him from his work, some undercutting his intuitive genius by coercing him into being analytical about his art. His reputation makes him vulnerable to those seeking his endorsement of causes about which he knows nothing. His work is gradually relegated to spare times and spare spaces. His success leads to his decline. He tries various means, alcohol and women among them, to flee his restricting circumstances. Louise, his wife, who has brought on some of the difficulty, is almost cast aside. She takes on a drowned, defeated look.

Finally intuiting the need for utter detachment, Jonas builds himself a make-shift garret above the family hallway and secludes himself for several days. The simple, but prodigious result of days of work is a grimy canvas with a single word on it.

That French word is "*solidaire*" or "*solitaire*"—the third consonant is not clearly a "d" or a "t"—"solidarity" or "solitarity" in English. The artist was driven in both directions: to solidarity with people; to the solitary pursuit of his artistry.

"The Artist at Work" is a humorous story with a serious moral for the artist. Other people—family, friends, and associates—are essential for the inspiration which stimulates a work. But those same people, in their admiration, solicitude, and over-attention, may be the cause of failure. The artist needs the stimulation, but not the obtrusive presence, of others.

Contraries and opposites appear in this story as in much of Camus's work. The juxtaposing of opposites—from beautiful setting/ugly poverty in the Kabyle to solidarity/solitarity in "The Artist at Work"—is a recurrent feature of Camus's thought and work.

The final scene of the story, with the artist sequestered in his improvised loft, detached from his family and the crowds of friends, resonates with a remark in his *Notebooks*. In them Camus said that he could be most content within the bare walls of a hotel room where he could write without distraction. But in France a writer's fame brings repeated requests for the writer's opinion, judgment, endorsement, or pronouncement on some issue or cause. Recognized as one willing to take unpopular stands, he was called upon to make judgments on matters with which he had little acquaintance. Camus felt beleaguered and unfairly put upon by such demands. Jonas reflects Camus's unhappy experience.

Camus's success as a writer came without great effort, many people claimed. Camus "could write without blotting a line," said Philip Thody, translator of *Notebooks, 1935-1942*. But Camus read extensively in preparation for writing *Caligula* and *The Plague*, though neither one was an historical work, and for *The Rebel*. A large worksheet sketching out parts of *The Rebel* is crisscrossed with changes and marks for restructuring. Indeed, in the *Notebooks,* Camus says that the great fault of many modern writers is their unwillingness to revise. So Camus's depiction of Jonas's effortless success is ironic commentary on his own career.

"The Guest," already considered, also connects with Camus's own life. Daru, a French schoolteacher living among Arab Algerians, feels at home in the bleakness of the high, rocky country of the school's site in Algeria. But when he's told to take an Arab accused of murder to jail he is caught between the two cultures. He believes in Arab, and not French, justice for the prisoner. But Balducci, constable and former friend of Daru, insists on Daru's cooperation. Daru does all he can to motivate and assist the prisoner to escape. But the man insists on going to the French prison.

When, back at the schoolhouse, Daru sees, "You handed over our brother. You will pay for this," written on the chalkboard, he is aware of the cruel misunderstanding. With Balducci on one side and the Arabs on the other, he stands in the vast landscape that he loves, and he realizes that he is alone.

This story analogically shows Camus in the French/Algerian tragedy of the fifties. He was very much the man between, calling for each side to grant that the other had some reason on its side, asking each to reduce the violence, to stop the killings, to work out a solution fair to both sides. But he was excoriated for this middle position. Both sides flailed away at him because he was committed to neither the one side nor the other.

People in between, people in the median—such are Camusian rebels. They affirm values for others by risking themselves, thus demonstrating the validity for humanity of the values defended. They consistently maintain the values which lucidity has taught them. They resist systems and elements of them advanced by partisans. They stand in the median between oppositional forces which are potentially destructive if unchecked.

"The Adulterous Woman" tells of a woman vaguely ill at ease in a situation which is dimly unsatisfying, though not deplorable. Janine is dully content in the bourgeois life led by her husband. Marcel supplies her basic needs, admires, and needs her. She does not fault the life or him who provides it for her. But on a journey through Algerian desert places she glimpses a harder, freer life enclosed within and responsive to the elemental forces of the world.

Through empty stretches of the land she experiences gritty sand, swirling wind—and the Arabs swathed against the chafing wind and sand, "free lords of a strange kingdom." Her bourgeois life depends in part on these with whom Marcel barters to gain the income which supports them. The Arab merchants who do not have to buy; the striding, arrogant man who forces Marcel to snatch his goods trunk out of the way—these things reveal her exile in a land where others are kings.

Then, driven by a force she cannot recognize, she entices Marcel to go along with her to the parapet where they overlook the empty kingdom. She drinks in a quality of life which staggers her. Marcel, too, is somehow touched by the unseen force which moves his wife.

Back at their hotel, after their evening meal, Janine enters the bed of her comfort and nestles against her husband's bourgeois warm back. Then, later in the night, noiselessly slipping from that warmth, she runs to the parapet in the darkness to rendezvous in the desert night. Under the star-filled sky, opened to the strange kingdom, she encloses the surging billows which the kingdom presses on her.

Her adultery consummated, she returns to her bed with Marcel. To his question about the cause of her silent crying, she murmurs, "Nothing." She could not tell him that she had overcome her exile through that chaste adultery on the parapet.

It is unlikely that Janine will renounce her life with Marcel in favor of the austere life of the desert. She will not replace her old life with a new one. But her life is renewed, and Marcel's life will be changed, if only subtly, by Janine's tryst with the desert kingdom.

This is not the story of a European woman swept off her feet, carried into the desert by a virile, lordly sheik. It is not romanticism. It is the story of a rebellious spirit. She dares to respond to the arousal coming from a vision of life beyond the boundaries of her experience.

Like Janine, Camus was immersed in the bourgeois world, though he had not begun there. His early lyrical writings attest to the appeal and strength of the lush barrenness of the land of sand and sea in Algeria. But he had more than glimpsed the other kingdom, for he was raised as a child within it. Outside the boundaries of that realm he felt he was in exile. But he did not abandon the new life he had entered. The other kingdom had enriched his present life, giving it depth and connection with life's elemental ground.

"The Growing Stone" has affinity with "The Adulterous Woman" in that both feature the prominence of environment and the atmosphere of place. Both Janine and D'Arrast are out of their home contexts in a strange land which is foreign and compelling. Each is privileged, well-provided for, yet subtly envious of the leaner life of those native to the land visited. Both experience mysterious union with people basically strange to them. Both find release from old restraints and a kind of new birth gained through rapport with people markedly different from them.

Janine had been in exile in her bourgeois life without knowing it, but D'Arrast deliberately exiled himself as he left Eu-

Gentle Vision and Vehement Irony 115

rope behind. He traveled to Brazil in quest of something he could not name. Janine, in unrecognized exile, consorted with a kingdom of which she would never be a part. But D'Arrast, conscious of his self-exile, achieved inclusion in the lowly kingdom he entered.

D'Arrast, a civil engineer, has come to Iguape, Brazil, to build a revetment against the river's flooding. It will most benefit the poorest people living in the native quarter. Though treated as a hero by the city's leaders, he initially feels a modicum of hostility when he visits the poor quarter where his good deed of construction will have the most effect. Yet it is in that neighborhood that he is to find such acceptance and fellow-feeling that his spirit will be transformed.

From a ship's cook with whom he has made contact, D'Arrast learns of the cook's vow to carry a heavy stone in the saint's day procession the next morning. The cook is going to fulfill a promise made to Jesus when he was shipwrecked and in fear of drowning. He promised to carry the heavy stone if he were saved. D'Arrast confesses that he wishes he could make such a promise, for he has come close to causing death by his fault. He'd like to find some way to atone.

That night the cook and the engineer attend the ritualistic, mesmeric dance of the natives. Beforehand, the cook asks D'Arrast to lead him away before he's danced so long that he'll be unable to fulfill his vow on the morrow. When the time comes to leave, however, the cook coolly sends the engineer off alone, and continues to dance.

Next day, D'Arrast observes the procession from a balcony above it. He sees the cook falter under the stone, then disappear from sight around a building. Some time later, when the cook reappears, deadened with fatigue under the rock of his vow, D'Arrast sees that he is at the point of exhaustion.

D'Arrast dashes from the balcony, shouldering through people in the procession. He comes alongside the cook, speaking words of encouragement. The cook staggers on. He's already fallen once under the load and now seems likely to fall again. As he weaves forward, the stone slips off his shoulder to the ground.

D'Arrast moves alongside the cook and stoops to sweep the stone off the ground. He hoists it onto his big shoulder and walks on toward the church. But then, without knowing why, he turns away from the church and walks toward the native quarter, ignoring the shouted protests of those in the procession. Alone in the quarter, he moves to the cook's hut, drops the stone into the still-smoldering fire pit, and stands, enveloped by a strange joy.

When he is quietly joined by members of the cook's family, they invite him to move into their circle around the stone and the fire. He is no longer an outsider.

This story, like "The Adulterous Woman," pits bourgeois culture against a "less-developed" culture in contest for the inner allegiance of a man. D'Arrast sets aside—leaves behind—the privileges of his own "advanced" country. The benefits, advantages, and complexities of urban life had left him unsatisfied, pulled away from the earth of our being. In Iguape, among the poor and poverty-stricken by the river, he was drawn into truer connection with that earth.

"The Growing Stone" affirms the values of the "less-privileged" life. D'Arrast was not poor, but he identified with the poor of Iguape. He turned away from the heavy impress of European civilization and found authentic life among those close to the soil and air of our sustenance. In the story he achieves detachment from the insulated life of advanced civilization. He finds the attachment of solidarity with those gathered around the fire of penury.

Metropolitan France with its pulsing Paris—where Camus lived—is a far remove from Brazil and Iguape, and probably preferred by most as domicile. But Camus's story contradicts the preference. Camus had briefly visited Brazil, so the setting was not unknown to him. In a piece called "A Macomba in Brazil," he described a dance like that in the short story. And he had lived the life of poverty himself. D'Arrast may be seen as Camus's proxy in Brazil.

Autobiographical elements and affirmation of protagonists are set aside for the telling of "The Renegade." It is told through the mouth of a monologist, letting the man depict himself. The vehemence of the telling is not insignificant testimony to the author's attitude toward his created character.

The context of the story is religious; the principal character is fanatically, primitively religious. So there is obvious, but not exclusive, religious import. In *The Rebel* Camus used the church, faith, and symbols of faith as metaphors for features of political or ideological groups. And so in "The Renegade."

The principal character is obstinate in nature. In early life he was toughened by physical hardship and the stern discipline of his parents. He was stubbornly proud of his physical toughness and hardness, and these were repeated in his hard-headedness. While still a boy he was recruited and trained for religious orders. In his training he laughingly accepted all the physical force required to insert the doctrine into his mind. Whether or not the faith was beat into him, the doctrine of the faith was. He gathered from this instructional method that it is by knocks and jolts that the power of the faith is manifested and applied.

Perhaps inevitably, he was attracted to that Africa mission area where the people were reputed to be the most fierce, the most resistant to the faith—the people of the city of salt.

Doubtless sensing some of his own characteristics among those attributed to the people who live in the city of salt, he wants to be sent on a mission to those people. But his superiors, recognizing their trainee's primitive and fatuous views, forbid him to undertake the missionizing of the salt city.

So he deputizes and dispatches himself. He steals money from the treasury and employs a guide. On the way, the guide relieves him of the money not yet spent. At the end of the trail the missioner enters the city of salt unbidden and unheralded.

Like a thoughtless latter-day Copernicus he intends to tilt the world into the Kingdom by prying the most resistant people into the faith. The rock-hardness of his faith, he believes, will enable him to endure whatever will come in his encounters with the fierce people. Success in that most difficult place, he believes, will lift and move the world.

Operating on such a premise, he is clearly not a rebel—one who seeks amelioration and mitigation. He's intent on establishing his beliefs over those of other people. He is a revolutionary who would impose one order over another.

But in the city of salt he meets his match. Hastily and cruelly imprisoned, he is left alone for a decade of days. Then applied and observed suffering are used by his captors as the evangelistic means to convert the renegade. He is made to bow before the Fetish. The power of his Lord is insufficient, at least in the renegade's hands, to withstand the power of the axe-headed Fetish and the merciless Sorcerer. Thoroughly impressed by the power wielded over him, he yields up his faith in favor of the Sorcerer's faith.

The renegade, when the reader meets him, has escaped and set himself in ambush to strike down the representative of his former faith, who is coming to rescue him. But he is a proselyte, as fanatic now for the faith of the Fetish as he had been for his old faith. He has met a power, a force, stronger than that which he had intended to apply to the people of salt.

Since his concept of religion is one of power and force, his allegiance to what's stronger is a logical outcome. He had started with the thought that God is power. Thus, when superior power fell upon him he gave it obeisance. His categorical thinking could lead to no other conclusion. The renegade responds to force: he is defeated by force; he puts his faith in the power which has forced him into submission. His primitive belief is easily replaced by a more primitive—and merciless—belief.

"The Renegade" is a grim story which lingers in the memory. There are scenes which trouble the senses and shudder the mind. The renegade is at once pitiable and pitiless. He asks for the trouble he gets yet nevertheless evokes some of our sympathy when he gets it. He swings from one position to the other, like the water in a photographer's tilting tray, with a sudden rush and surge from one end to the other. Once tipped, he is a settled extremist, stolid and unchanging, oblivious to thoughts other than those which support his conclusions. Yet when circumstances bring him to a fall he rushes rapidly, cataclysmically to the opposite stand.

Whether at one extreme or the other the renegade was totally involved, totally engaged in what had caught his spirit—blind to nuance, to subtlety, to fineness of discrimination.

The renegade is grotesquely displayed in this story, but he is to be found in those hyperbolic folk who must go all out at the end of one limb or another. If the chosen limb cracks, the one poised there is likely to climb pellmell to the end of a limb on the opposite side of the tree.

The similarity between the fanatically religious and the revolutionary mind is obvious. This extreme inconstancy springs from the constancy of the absolutist, the revolutionary, attitude. Here in the midst of some gentle stories Camus has told a shattering parable of the revolutionary mind and spirit.

The Fall was originally a part of *Exile and the Kingdom*. But it outgrew its beginning and was published separately. Like "The Renegade," The Fall is both a monologue and a social critique. Like Meursault of *The Stranger*, Jean-Baptiste Clamence is a loner.

Meursault, in the midst of a people of pedestrian and indiscriminate morality, is a man without an ethic, condemned by a people with a faulty ethic. He elicits our sympathy not by his admirability but by evoking our reaction against the hypocritical ethic of those who do him in. He is a stranger among people with whom we do not want to identify.

Clamence exhibits a super ethic in the midst of—and above—a people impressed by altruism, though not inclined to it themselves. He believes that his ethic is fully realized. In truth he's over-developed it for the impression of people who shrug at ethics. He self-consciously incarnates those virtues to which others only give lip service. Clamence is a loner in the midst of a people remarkably like ourselves.

When the reader meets him, Clamence appears as a lawyer who has achieved excellence in self-esteem. He enjoys such happiness that he believes it authorized by some higher decree. He excels physically, he excels professionally. In love and in reputation he is excellent. He has discovered a natural resource for altruism—the put-upon, the defenseless, the paupered widow—whom he represents legally. He extracts profit from championing unprofitable cases. Everything makes him feel good about himself.

He is a man with a clear image of the good and a high image of himself vis-a-vis that good. He satisfies his own high ideal. Yet beneath his recitation of excellence appears a contrapuntal line of irony. To excel in grieving, in modesty, and in self-effacing is hyperbolic hypocrisy. Clamence, busy living his life, doesn't hear the contrapuntal score, although it sounds, latently and implicitly, along with the dominant notes of professed virtuosity.

The counter theme first surfaces strongly, briefly, at midnight, in the rain, in the middle of a bridge over the wide Seine. He glimpses an attractive female figure leaning—was it dejectedly—on the railing above the water. After a moment of onward walking, he hears a splash and a cry—was the cry one of fear or of release? He freezes into immobility. He who majored in succoring the unfortunate is now unable—or unwilling—to initiate a rescue. He does nothing. Careful inattention to the newspapers for the next few days allows him to suppress and submerge that haunting theme of irony for another two or three years.

A long time later the tragic cry on the one bridge translates into a derisive cry on another. This time, in full daylight, surveying the Ile de la Cité, splendid heart of a wondrous city, Clamence feels his full grandeur. Face to face with the Vert Galant, Henri Quatre, King worthy of the title of His Majesty, Clamence swells in chesty pride. But at the height of fullest inspiration the fullness is punctured by a laugh. The river, the bridge, the island all are empty of anything that could have emitted that laugh. Except for Clamence himself. Though he knows, tacitly, that he is the source of laughter he cannot bring that knowledge to the surface—not yet. But he who had mounted the heights has fallen down, whether he grants it or not.

Later, the private slippage on the bridge is replicated by a public downfall in the paltry setting of a traffic incident. There, bested by a nobody, the great altruist is spurred to revenge, but misses the essential moment. He feels the mantle of greatness fall off his shoulders, noisily.

After these incidents he takes corrective action, somewhat like Jonas, in trying to muzzle or obliterate the laughter. His incessant attempts to quell it—if we're to believe all his stories—lead him to excessive use of alcohol, to debauchery, to raucous engagement in radical philosophy, to attempted heroism in war. But there is no cure. As antidote to a delusional sense of excellence Clamence takes on a pathological sense of guilt.

His lawyer's career of noble cases had not manifested nobility—nor did his failure to rescue constitute true guilt. As he had exaggerated his nobility, so he produced an extravagant case of uncalled-for guilt. Anyone with a realistic sense of his own capacity and worth would have felt regret and sadness, but certainly not guilt, over the first incident on the bridge.

The things Clamence holds against himself are thoroughly rational reasons for not launching rescue. Any lawyer would count them off readily—and he claimed to be a lawyer. The rain and the darkness of the night would have prevented his seeing the woman in the water; a run downstream would have left him breathless, with reduced capacity to swim; and the young woman—if she had fallen by choice—might very well have resented his interference in her suicide, had he attempted it. Surely his responsibility would be to alert the police, who must have responded to such cases before. But that would have been to admit that he was helpless. . . . His guilt—stemming from his failure to fulfill the inflated vision of his own greatness—is as distorted as his self-perception.

The multiplicity of religious symbolism evoked by Clamence serves as a smoke screen—maybe for himself as well as for his complacent auditors—to obscure the reality of the falseness of his guilt.

All the religious symbolism Clamence uses is bent to a contrary purpose. Baptism is bitter—condemning, rather than cleansing. The receptacle of the Zuider Zee is the "holy font" in which the speck of guilt floats to Clamence. The birds—representative of the Holy Spirit—are eternally frustrated in their search for heads on which to light, every one as unwilling and as unworthy as he. Yes—Clamence's previous exalted sense of worth is matched by a degraded sense of the possibility of release from guilt.

This man, a "false prophet for shabby times," is a model for the come-uppance of smugness. Those with an inflated sense of their own importance, worth, significance, and soteriological capacity, are the most impervious to the saving potential of anything outside themselves. He with a distended sense of self seizes the chance to make another person wallow in the guilt he projects.

The inflated personality is deeply troubled by the smallest perforation. That small leak is exquisitely fatal. No vulcanization can patch it. The only option for the false prophet is to aim his slow leak at compliant listeners, with the hope that the fetid air will persuade them that they are more guilty than the leaker.

Clamence is in great contrast to Janine and D'Arrast in *Exile and the Kingdom*. They are authentic searchers for life. They achieve something positive, a brief vision of a kingdom, a kind of rebirth. Both take steps to attach themselves to the mysterious life to which they are attracted. Theirs are forward movements to meet whatever their openness discovers. Alongside them, roguishly attractive as he is, Clamence measures up as a thoroughly genuine bogus character. False by his own fabrication, Clamence is authentically depicted by Camus.

Jean-Baptiste Clamence, who calls for repentance as did the biblical John the Baptizer, is a noisy brayer. His surname epitomizes the duplicity which he readily admits. "Clamence" appears to be an amalgam of *clameur*, empty noise, and *clemence*, grace and mercy. He hints that he is an evangelist concerned for the salvation of his willing hearer. But he also hints that he is a charlatan bent on elevating himself above his chastened listener.

This devious character, alongside the sterling personages of Janine and D'Arrast, is certainly not designed to call us to be judge-penitents, bogus as that is, or to prepare us for the acceptance of a faith which may follow upon conviction of the need for repentance. Jean-Baptiste Clamence is not meant for emulation. He is companion to the renegade—one to be avoided—for the Clamences of the world claim to show us the way by virtue and contrition. But in them neither way is genuine. One stems from a feeling of vast superiority and the other from the horror of falling short of supposed greatness.

There are autobiographic features in *The Fall*. But they are ironic and hyperbolic. Clamence does reflect something of Camus—and of what others claimed to be true of him. Camus had been called a moralist and a man of overarching pride; a man who held himself aloof and above reproach; a man who refused to participate in movements directed by others, and who was perennially critical of the actions of such movements; a man who was something of a womanizer; a critic of religious leaders' pronouncements.

In reference to his identity as a moralist Camus had once said, "If I were to rape my grandmother in a public park it would be called a moral act." And the irony of this remark is elevated in *The Fall*. "Yes," Camus is saying, "you're right. Here is my portrait—and yours—a man of his times."

Exile and the Kingdom may have come from a tired hand, as Roger Quilliot suggests in *Théâtre, Récits, Nouvelles*, but that hand formed authentic Yvars, Janine, Daru, Jonas, and D'Arrast. It also gave us the steadily absolutist renegade for warning. And, grown to be more than a short story, it produced *The Fall* and Jean-Baptiste Clamence, the genuinely false advocate of fake penitence. The tired hand created gems for the reader's perplexity and reflection.

VII

The Rebellious Stance

Rebellion and rebellious thought are the strings on which Camus's essays and fictional works can be hung, without implication of linearity. They comprise a circle of connectedness more than a system of thought. They show a habit rather than a program.

The gems on the cords cast more rays and colors than those here offered, of course. This book offers an overview, not an exhaustive commentary (which could fill volumes.) Furthermore, *The Rebel*, Camus's major philosophical work, is full of reference and allusion not readily accessed by Americans, although *The Myth of Sisyphus* is not so trammeling. However, the themes found in *The Myth* and *The Rebel* glow in the imaginative works of fiction and drama, where the irrational and nostalgia are only implicit, but rebellion is explicit, though rarely violent.

The Myth, Caligula, and *The Stranger* come from the same time period. *The Rebel* was contemplated even as *The Myth* was being written. Thus Sisyphus, Meursault, Caligula, and Cherea, by contrast and advancement, were given their heads to lead the way to Dora Brilliant and Ivan Kaliayev.

Camus's works emerged in a time of unsettledness, when old acceptances were questioned and often rejected. Old truths suffered abandonment. Philosophers, religionists, and ideologues confidently offered clarity in face of the irrational, presenting their thoughts as the truth. Many people accepted what was proffered, apparently satisfied. Others gave up the search. They contented themselves with less than full satisfaction.

In reality, the truth cannot be found, though the search must not end. Offerers and accepters of "the truth" are both deluded. Yet lucid people never lose their zeal, never cease the quest for the sweet water of clarity, though the murkiness of the universe continues.

The stories and dramas of Camus are complex, often ambiguous. In the skein, from the beginning, one thought persists: Humans, though sustained within it, are mystified by the universe in which they find themselves. They seek clarity as the mythical Tantalus sought water. They stretch out for clarity.

Camus's characters variously recognize their Tantalus-like condition. Some are on the alert, seeking rebirth into fuller living. Some experience a fleeting moment of at-one-ness with the life around them. Some are in extremis, aware or becoming aware both of what is and of what might be, in search of their true selves and their true places in a universe which gives both pleasure and pain. And many are in that severe state of unrest or ennui called the absurd. In experiencing or confronting suffering to the point of death, they discover the profound value of living.

For Camus those most aware of the stand-off between nostalgia and the irrational are cognizant of the universe as it is. The absurd stance maintains that tension and has validity for the lone individual. Humans are rarely alone, however, and the absurd stance, with its consequences of quantity, freedom, and revolt, does not serve social humans. The stance is basically deficient in failing to recognize that there are others with the same right as the absurd ones to fullness of life. When quantity and freedom are exploited in life, especially by powerful people, human solidarity is injured or denied. Lives are adversely affected. The absurd stance does not serve humanity well.

Humans, when fully human (and there are those who act as if they are not), have need of values to live by, in order to be authentic. A faint knowledge of true human nature lies in the spirit of everyone, even if it is known only in an implicit, subconscious, tacit way. Assaults against that human nature, impositions upon it, molestations of it may be abided for a time, but eventually they lead to rebelling, whether inwardly suppressed or outwardly actualized. In actualizing rebellion, rebellers lift up a human value, for others more than for themselves, since they risk themselves in rebelling.

Rebellion may be metaphysical, but more often issues from human/human relations. Rebellion is at once an affirmation of human nature and a rejection of those systems or orders which oppress; and here Camus's thought has the widest implication: Imposed order is not to be passively endured.

His fictional work features conscious rebels who oppose oppression. They are lucid people in urgent search for further clarity. They press for the reformation of government and regimes, despite the certain knowledge that any order created by humans leaves the irrational largely intact. They oppose those humans who oppress by constructions which "order" life. Rebels oppose any but the minimal order needed to insure a social climate in which there are no obstacles to each human's right to be a human.

Those acquainted with the life and personal influence of Camus discover that his attitudinal stance is firmly rebellious in the constructive way described in *The Rebel*. His singular humanity is revealed by his sympathetic understanding of little people, evidenced by *L'Envers et L'Endroit* and *Exile and the Kingdom*; his championing of workers' causes; his identification with the victims of repressive regimes; and his utterly persuasive essay against capital punishment in "Reflections on the Guillotine" in *Resistance, Rebellion, and Death*.

Camus's life and his works corroborated one another. There is something of the legendary about the man who was derisively called "the little Christ" by some of those who observed and objected to his high moral consciousness. The appellation is remarked and discredited by an associate, a proof-reader for Editions Gallimard, in *A Albert Camus, ses amis du Livre*. The mythic quality is recalled in this little book of remembrances put together by the printers, typists, typesetters, composers, and editorial staff of Gallimard.

The tears of a Parisian bookseller, four years after Camus's unexpected death, repeated the tribute, as did the testimony of Edmond Charlot, who said that he and his Paris friends asked themselves, when facing critical issues, "What would Camus say?" These words of associates and fellow-writers, several years after his death, continually reemphasize one point: Camus was a rare spirit as well as a rare talent.

A durable, stoic softness of heart permeated the life of this rebellious thinker. For the most part Camus saw those who opposed him not so much as opponents, antagonists, or adversaries as victims of their own propensity for order, and thereby partially blinded to reality.

Far from the popular understanding of the rebel as a nihilistic subverter of law and justice, Camus described the rebel as one who searches out and lifts up emergent values in a time marked by the absence of eternal values. In the hands of Camus, rebellion and the rebel are agents, not of decimation and destruction, but of discovery and affirmation.

Rebellion and lucidity serve a reforming function, breaking up the crust of systems and orders which enslave human minds and lives. Whereas ordered and straight thinking propagate and preserve themselves, rebellious thought looks for contraries and contradiction. It thereby cleanses, renews, and reforms itself, keeping its practitioners from settled contentment with presumptive positions. Rebellious thought rises from the contraries exposed by lucidity; lucidity maintains rebellious thought.

Lucidity links thought and feeling to produce reasoning—as distinct from reason. Reason is imperialistic and tyrannical, insisting on the supremacy of logic and deductive thought. It is ordered thinking, preferring logical validity to the nonlogical evidences of feeling. Lucidity issues in thought rebelling against itself.

Impelled by the twin realities of nostalgia and the irrational, rebellious thought critiques itself, doubles back on itself, looks again from another perspective at what it has said, in order to avoid the hazard of straight thinking, with its obstinate, dangerous tendency to authenticate itself.

Rebellious thought knows and honors limits. And it understands that thought can discover truths, but never Truth. It therefore lets itself run to track down a truth, knowing full well that another scent will lead to another truth. Rebellious thought comprehends that truths contradict one another and that Truth is not fully discoverable. It is the clash of thoughts, the encounter of truths upon which rebellious thought relies for its veracity.

Lucidity and rebellion are valuable in various arenas, from basic human relations to religious thinking. Camus had profound religious sensitivity, though he was not a believer. Nor, despite suggestions by some readers of *The Fall*, was he en route to religious belief. The testimony of close associates is persuasive on this point. Yet Camus's work is so evocative of religious response that his work can be said to have religious import.

The Fall is replete with religious symbols. It was probably prelude to yet another set of fiction/essays, on human nature. Camus had indicated that a work underway, already titled *The First Man*, would feature a man in the pristine state of pure rawness, untouched by culture, creed, or ideology—an unalloyed piece of humanity who could be examined for the essence of human nature. The central character of this work was to be a man carrying that real human nature. Since the essential core of a human is frequently betrayed by the quality of our living, it can be assumed that the First Man would be shown discovering true human nature. For Camus often talked of the need for rebirth, for renaissance, for becoming what we essentially are, for fully realizing our humanity.

The First Man, as published by Camus's daughter in 1994, is really only a first sketch of the intended novel. As is, it is a partial autobiography—the story of Camus's boyhood. It would have had to have undergone substantial reworking to change into the story of a pristine, unmolded human being.

Rebellious thought, at first attention, does not seem to promise much for religious thinkers. These thinkers begin with a premise—that there is a God, that God is approachable, that God is concerned with the affairs of humans, and that God has revealed Godself (in the Muslim, as well as in the Judeo-Christian tradition).

Religious thought, then, appears to be in the lineage of straight thinking: Begin with the truth of God, extend, amplify, and expand that truth deductively to draw the religious conclusions. Or begin with a religious proposition and address hearers by means of the devices of straight thinking: attaching to the proposition all those bits and particles from life, literature, culture, and human nature which prove the chosen propositional truth. Much, if not most preaching (Christian, at least) proceeds on just such a basis. Preachers have become advocates, demonstrators, explicators of the truth they profess.

Believers may quail at the idea of lucidity, with its ideal of stasis between nostalgia and the irrational, but they know that they are not dealing with certainty. Kierkegaard's theologizing sprang from the insight that faith in God is not based on objective certainty. Faith is a wager upon which the faithful base their lives. The faithful stake much upon that wager and at their best forgo those gratifications which are at the expense of others. Religious thinking and discourse which acts as though based on certainty may be persuasive, but it is not faithful to the truth.

The faith stance need not be at the cost of blindness to the realities of the world. Indeed, the saints of faith are those most aware of the world's sufferings, their own or that of others, yet they still maintain their faith. They have not let nostalgia suppress their awareness of the irrational. The yearning to see clearly has not obstructed their perception of disorder, suffering, and the reign of death.

Believers need not accept the scheme of things with docile tranquility. Those who work to alleviate the human suffering caused by natural catastrophes may demonstrate their lucidity. They lucidly face the contraries of tragedy and calamity in a world they believe to be good. They maintain their commitment in the face of tragic paradox. The priest, Father Paneloux, in *The Plague*, reveals Camus's recognition of the existence of such believers.

The constancy of religiously faithful people does not obscure the fact that religious belief is a postulate, a wager that Truth has been revealed, if only partially. Lucidity shows believers that the faith materials of scripture and tradition are of mixed quality, shaped by numerous and varied minds. Nostalgia urges believers to search Truth behind the faint reflections of it contained in faith materials. Acknowledgement of the unfathomability of the universe—the product of lucid awareness—leads believers to concede that they have many portions of truth, though not Truth itself.

Rebellious religious thinkers seek further sightings of their own while they honor and attend to the thoughts of others who also seek the Truth. But they understand that Truth is too vast, complex, and mysterious to be encapsulated by an infinite number of human minds. They repeatedly try, therefore, to search out Truth through multiple, and largely tentative, sorties into the unknown, the unplumbable. They make essays, in the original meaning of the word, for their own discovery and for the lucid thinking of others. They believe that it is in the interface between various understandings and explications of religious meaning that Truth is most closely approached. In the stance of lucidity, they practice rebellious thinking in religion.

In the context of the modern state. rebellious thought seems to have an inherent, substantial weakness. Lucid rebels forgo accession to the seat of power, leaving operation of a system, and initiatives within that system, to those who have inherited, devised, or produced the system. Rebels seem thus to play into the hands of systematizers and governors—and to dictators, right or left, at the worst.

Mass communications and armed force enhance the power of governments. The powers of the modern state grow ever stronger. Power has to be respected, but not necessarily honored, and the nostalgia of the governed for order leads them, even though reluctantly, to support their governors. Governance may thus become excessive, the excess coming slowly, imperceptibly, like failing brakes on a car. When the hazard is fully recognized, it is too late to guard against the danger. Governors with the most benevolent of motives may thus become oppressors.

The possessor of power may seek justice, but any who question the application of that justice, even without malice, can be perceived as adversaries, and pressure for change may be interpreted as a threat. Self-preservation and a felt need to strengthen the governor's powers, out of belief that others will seek to displace or oust the leader, stimulates an ever more formidable defense of that order.

Rebels or revolutionaries, the inevitable products of establishment, challenge the consolidated order. Both may have worthy motives; but they are differentiated by their goals: Rebels seek mitigation or reformation; revolutionaries strive to displace and replace the government.

Without a widely supported tradition of power transfer on some regular basis, attempted seizure of power is an ever-present likelihood. Risks for the challenger are considerable, however, and, with the entrenched power of the modern state, are likely to become even greater. Hence, the role of rebels in the Camusian mode will become ever more needed and viable. Though philosophically opposed to the seizing of power, they are convinced that every order needs correcting. Aware of the dangers of becoming protectionists, rather than correctors, they shun power and the direction of affairs. They search out the means for enjoining those in power to move toward a more just society.

The nonviolent methods of Mahatma Gandhi and Martin Luther King, Jr. resonate with Camusian rebellion and serve the rebel well. Rebels limit themselves to suasive means unless the situation becomes so desperate that violence is the only recourse. In that extremity the rebels will reluctantly turn to force—but to the absolute minimum degree necessary, and only for the purpose of forcing change in the system.

In the political life of the United States, Camusian rebellion might well work within the political center, standing apart from the two major parties, and seeking to influence the policies and programs of both. It would not organize to administer a government, but would content itself with watchdogging the party in power and in influencing the actions of the challengers. Currently, Common Cause, the Concord Coalition, and The League of Women Voters are organizations which appear to incorporate features of the rebellious ideal.

A politics of the rebellious center will be faulted for being reactive and never constructive. But correction is constructive when it rights error. While others will exercise direction of power, rebels will act to humanize political structures and practices. Abstaining from power-holding will be deliberate, springing from the conviction that power-holders are advocates and defenders by necessity, and thereby blinded to the constant need for reformation. Camusian rebels will provide the impetus for pressuring power-wielders into revision and adjustment.

Camusian rebellion does not threaten the extinction of governors. There is no danger that the world will ever run out of power-people. Humans through the centuries have sought and exercised power. There will always be the systematizers, the orderers, the power-appliers to be rebelled against, to be forced to reformation, to be pushed to provide a fuller justice in a more just society. With nostalgia exercising its imperial sway over the minds and wills of humans there will be an abundance of governors, with concomitant need for rebels to keep them just.

The general tendency and temper of humans may be the most critical of the needs to which rebellious thought is responsive. Humans today seem strongly oriented to for or against, to a "yes" or a "no." Propositional thinking depends on two-valued response: affirmative or negative. Propositional thought and the two-valued orientation have their place in courts of law and in legislative assemblies—in arenas, that is, where both sides recognize that each presents a weighted version of the evidence involved.

Interchanges under such conditions occur face to face, in the main, in the presence of all participants. Common attendance reduces exaggerations and distortions, since rebuttal is right at hand. But this feature does not always safeguard the truth, as observers of trials and of governing assemblies—from the village to the UN—fully realize. For deliberate and willful misuse of evidence and argument persist. But at least the corrective of the other voice is heard.

However, presence-before-one-another is not common in many areas—in journalism, in the cold war, in propaganda, and in disagreements between people separated from one another by borders and other political barriers. In every human, it seems, there are inclinations to take advantage of another, to aggrandize one's self. Thus one is led to slant and exaggerate in order to gain. When matters escalate, the stakes mount and winning becomes imperative. Allies are sought and appealed to. Eventually, without intervention from outside, the definitive stance of side-taking may stretch to giant height and the situation become fully polarized. Those who began as disagreers have become enemies. And enemies are fit subjects for violence in word and act.

Somewhere, some time in the prehistory of a lethal showdown a premise or a proposition has been avowed. Consciously or not, someone else has taken the opposite position. At some point or other, when the other side is personalized, each becomes an advocate and begins to accrue all the positive evidence supporting his position. An accumulation of mass is piled up, leading each advocate to an even stronger belief that right is on his side. Similar construction on the other side leads to identical certainty about opposite contentions.

The two-valued orientation emanating from propositional and straight thinking, in extreme extension, is violent and murderous. It appears to solve things only by the expedient of exhausting one side or the other. Instead of seeking out points of agreement by which a mutually acceptable compromise can be reached, programmed or straight thinkers commit excess. In amassing the means to prove the rightness of their claims, they are forced to extreme means, in desperate occasions, to prove that rightness.

The insistence on developing, supporting, defending, proclaiming, and asserting one's absolute convictions has inevitable consequences. It drives one to pile up evidence, opinion, testimony—and force, in capital issues—to support that position. It leads also to the search for weaknesses, inconsistencies, and wrongness on the part of opponents. The "against or for" stance divides outsiders into allies or enemies. The extreme extension of such a process is the vendetta or war. And war spawns enemies beyond and traitors within. As long as humans pursue straight thinking, with its yes or no, there will be aggravations leading to violence and escalations leading to war.

In worst-case scenarios advocates become opponents and the amassing of support accelerates. With one's own rightness assumed, the errors of the opposition are accumulated. Soon these errors become faults, and blemishes of character and person may be added to the fractures marked in the other's reasoning. At highest pitch an opponent become an enemy and a fit subject for forceful correction.

From the disagreement and growing bitterness of divorce proceedings to the animosities and wars of nations, the pattern is the same. Once the two-valued orientation is accepted, in association with propositional thought and straight thinking, people are caught up in a sense of rightness and wrongness, by yes and no, by the eventual willingness to subdue or defeat the opponent.

Camusian rebels stand between, in the median, between the yes and the no. Camusian rebels know the temptation to engage in fatal embrace with those who see things differently. Camusian rebels will dare to say that there is virtue and vice in each of the opposing phalanxes. Camusian rebels will expect to receive the jibes, taunts, and attacks of those who demand a negative or an affirmative. Camusian rebels, lucid rebels, know that humans have life in common and that all are brothers and sisters before they are enemies, that there is more to draw them together than to drive them apart.

* * * * *

In the middle of the bitter French-Algerian controversy, Camus's activities corroborated his writings. Believing that there was right and wrong on each side, Camus aligned himself with neither, and was condemned by both. For failing to support its position he was accused, by each side, of being on the side of the other.

In the bitter argument-by-killing Camus was the man in the median, subject to assault by both. Yet his was the humane position. He affirmed that each side had the right to live. He sought to reduce the hostility, to remove the weapons of assault, to get the two sides to recognize what they commonly believed, to negotiate about those things which split them apart.

In his "Preface to Algerian Reports" (found in *Resistance, Rebellion, and Death*), Camus wrote, "Here is a group of selected articles and texts concerning Algeria . . . spaced out over a period of twenty years . . . until 1958. . . . These texts sum up the position of a man who . . . cannot approve a policy of preservation or oppression in Algeria . . . [or] a policy of surrender that would abandon the Arab people to an even greater misery, [and] tear the French in Algeria from their century-old roots. . . ."

The articles were drawn from a series he'd written outlining a temperate position for resolving the French-Algerian conflict. Included is "Appeal for a Civil Truce," which Camus delivered in Algiers on January 22d, 1956. The appeal had the initial support of some Arab Algerians, but rightists demonstrated outside the meeting hall. Though the demonstration was threatening, it was inconsequential, and applause rewarded Camus inside. But the side-takers in the conflict were firmly set, giving little hope for change.

The appeal had no measurable success. Camus stood almost alone.

It cannot be promised that rebellious thought will be "successful" and solve all the problems of the world. But rebellious thought—and Camusian rebels—far from being threats to society, are the mode of thought and agents of change which offer hope for turning humanity away from its fatal tendencies.

Camus has bequeathed the world a legacy of lucidity.

Bibliography

Periodicals:

Alger-Républicain, May-June 1939, Algiers, Algeria.
Situation, I, 1947, Gallimard, Paris.
Soir-Républicain, October-December 1939, Algiers, Algeria.

Works by Albert Camus

Caligula and Three Other Plays, Stuart Gilbert, translator. Vintage, New York, 1946.
Essais, Roger Quilliot et Louis Faucon, annotateurs. Gallimard et Calmann-Levy, Paris, 1965.
The Fall and Exile and the Kingdom, Justin O'Brien, translator. Modern Library, New York, 1956, 1957.
The First Man, David Hapgood, translator. Alfred A. Knopf, New York, 1995.
Lyrical and Critical Essays, Philip Thody, editor, Ellen Conroy Kennedy, translator. Vintage, New York, 1968.
The Myth of Sisyphus, Justin O'Brien, translator. Vintage, New York, 1955.
Notebooks, 1935-1942, Philip Thody, translator. Alfred A. Knopf, New York, 1963.
Notebooks, 1942-1951, Justin O'Brien, translator. Alfred A. Knopf, New York, 1965.
The Plague, Stuart Gilbert, translator. Modern Library, New York, 1948.
Le Premier Homme. Gallimard, Paris, 1994.
The Rebel, Anthony Bower, translator. Vintage, New York, 1956.
Resistance, Rebellion, and Death, Justin O'Brien, translator. Modern Library, New York, 1960.
The Stranger, Stuart Gilbert, translator. Vintage, New York, 1946.
Théâtre, Récits, Nouvelles, Roger Quilliot, annotateur. Gallimard, Paris, 1962.

Books about Albert Camus:

A Albert Camus, ses amis du Livre, Roger Grenier, editor. Gallimard, Paris, 1962.
Albert Camus, Herbert R. Lottman. George Braziller, Inc., New York, 1980.
Albert Camus, a Life, Olivier Todd, Benjamin Ivry, translator. Alfred A. Knopf, New York, 1997.

handicapped physically, and I traveled worldwide for a number of years.

The company most popular is **Flying Wheels** (143 W. Bridge, St., Box 382, Owatonna, MN 55060; phone 800/535-6790). This company has specialized since 1970 in tours for the handicapped. For instance, in 1999 they offered trips to France, Italy, Egypt, Austria and Switzerland as well as cruises on the Princess line.

Regarding cruising, **World Wide Cruises** (8059 W. McNab Rd., Ft. Lauderdale, FL 33321; phone 800/882-9000 or visit *www.wwcruises.com*) has a brochure on "Cruising for the Physically Challenged" that ranks the various lines and ships by wheelchair accessibility. It's a useful planning tool.

In addition, all airlines, in compliance with the American Disabilities Act of 1990 (as amended), are required to have provisions for the handicapped when flying equipment set up for more than 19 passengers.

Should any readers desire more detailed information, they are welcome to write to me.

MARTIN SYDEN, 2557 Emory Dr. W., West Palm Beach, FL 33415

Get into group therapy.

Book a Gate 1 Travel escorted tour to Egypt, Morocco or Israel and relax.

At Gate 1, we take care of everything. Including you. Gate 1 guides are knowledgeable. Sightseeing itineraries are all-inclusive. Hotels are centrally located, putting you in the heart of everything. You'll get the most travel value at the best possible price.

Complete packages with air

to **Egypt**	fr $1789	pp
to **Morocco**	fr $1249	pp
to **Israel**	fr $1739	pp

More of the world for less.

So get ready to go.
Call your travel agent, or 800-682-3333.

GATE 1
T R A V E L
www.gate1travel.com
101 Limekiln Pike Glenside, PA 19038

Call for free brochures

Accessible Journeys, Inc. (35 West Sellers Ave., Ridley Park, PA 19078; phone 800/846-4537, fax 610/521-6959 or visit *www.disability travel.com*). Offers a multitude of tours "for the slow-walker, wheelchair and special-needs traveler."

Empress Directions Unlimited (123 Green Ln., Bedford Hills, NY 10507; phone 800/533-5343, fax 914/241-0243, e-mail *cruisesusa@aol.com* or visit *www.travel-cruises.com*). This travel agency makes arrangements for people with disabilities and has done a tour for blind travelers.

Flying Wheels Travel (143 W. Bridge St., Box 382, Owatonna, MN 55060; phone 800/535-6790, e-mail *thq@ll.net* or visit *www.fyingwheels travel.com*). A travel agency and tour operator for travelers with disabilities.

Holidays for You and Me (Swn Y Don, Morawel Close, Croesgoch, Pembrokeshire, SA62 5JS, Wales; e-mail *sian@jpmarketing.co.uk* or visit *www.jpmarketing.co.uk/holi days* — attn: Sian Hughes). Offers self-catering tours in the U.K. and Ireland for disabled travelers.

Nautilus Tours & Cruises (22567 Ventura Blvd., Woodland Hills, CA 91364; phone 800/797-6004

rangements for them in Italy and France.

Wheelchair Travel (1 Johnston Green, Guilford, Surrey GU2 6XS, U.K.; phone +44 [0] 1483 233640, fax +44 [0] 1483-23772, e-mail *info@ wheelchair-travel.co.uk* or visit *www. wheelchair-travel.co.uk*). Arranges independent travel for wheelchair travelers in the U.K., solo or in small groups.

NEWSLETTERS & BOOKS

The newsletter *Very Special Traveler* by Beverly Nelson is pub-

WEBSITES

www.fhwa.dot.gov is a site that lists laws, agencies and advocacy groups concerned with access to transportation.

www.access-able.com is the site for **Access-Able Travel Source** (Box 1796, Wheat Ridge, CO 80034; phone 303/232-2979) and lists travel agents who specialize in disabled travel.

www.jsrd.or.jp/dinf_us/disability resources/travel.htm is the site of **Disability Travel & Recreation Resources** with links to all kinds of travel information and accommodation information.

www.everybody.co.uk has listings for travel services and accommodations that are accessible for the disabled. Includes links and an airline directory.

www.mossresourcenet.org/travel. htm has travel links galore for tips and resources for disabled travelers.

www.raileurope.com/us is a site for information on accessible train travel in France and Europe (phone 800/456-RAIL).

MISCELLANEOUS

Deaf Access International (350

Everything for Language

- Audio Courses
- Video Courses
- Software Courses
- Travel Phrase Books
- Hand-held Translators
- Dictionaries and more!

Prepare BEFORE you leave!

Check out our HUGE selection of foreign language materials. Call today toll-free for FREE expert advice.

1-800-622-3574

Language Quest • 308 State • Los Altos, CA 94022

Shop our Online Catalog
www.LanguageQuest.com

Agencies and information sources for travelers with disabilities

After some initial requests for information on cruise lines and tour companies amenable to travelers with disabilities, *ITN* printed some reader responses in the magazine. Subsequently, more readers sent in suggestions, spurring the following additions. These listings are only samplings of the many agencies and information sources that handicapped travelers may wish to consult to plan or arrange trips.

Our thanks go to Josephine Detert of Largo, FL, and LaVerne Meyering of St. Louis, MO, for their input. Readers with further recommendations are welcome to write in.

TOUR OPERATORS & TRAVEL AGENCIES

Access First Travel (239 Commercial St., Malden, MA 02148; phone 800/557-2047 or 781/322-1610 or e-mail *accessfir@aol.com*). Makes cruise-ship arrangements for disabled travelers (also ground and air arrangements in the U.S. (See below: Roll Around Britain).

Accessible Italy (Regency San Marino, Via Ventotto Luglio 124, 47031 Borgomaggiore, Republica di San Marino; phone +390549-875392, fax +390549-907189, e-mail *info@accessibleitaly.com* or visit *www.accessibleitaly.com*). Offers group and individual tours in Italy for travelers, or in CA, 818/591-3159, or e-mail *willibingo@msn.com*). Tour operator and travel agency for people with disabilities. Sets up packages, mostly in Europe, and cruises. Arranges independent trips all over.

Navyo Nepal (e-mail *navyo@dnet.it*, attn: Navyo Bier, or visit *www.navyonepal.com*). Offers tours in Tibet and Bhutan for disabled travelers.

Roll Around Britain/Dale's Discovery (239 Commercial St., Malden, MA 02148; phone 866/382-8728 or 781/322-8197, e-mail *rabital@worldnet.att.net* or visit *www.dalesdiscovery.co.uk*). Offers escorted tours in the U.K. and Ireland for dis- lished six times a year and gives recommendations and travel tips for disabled travelers. $25 per year. Contact *Very Special Traveler*, Box 756, New Windsor, MD 21776; call 410/635-2881.

The quarterly magazine *Open World* is published by the Society for the Advancement of Travelers with Handicaps (SATH), 347 Fifth Ave. #610, New York, NY 10016; phone 212/447-7284, fax 212/725-8253 or visit *www.sath.org*.

Twin Peaks Press (Box 129, Vancouver, WA 98666; phone 800/637-2256) has several books, including "Directory of Travel Agencies for the Disabled" ($19.95), "Travel for

Bay St., PMB 255, San Francisco, CA 94133; phone 415/434-4008, fax 775/415-8625 or e-mail *info@deafaccessintl.org* or visit *www.deafaccessintl.org*). Advocates for better travel services and industry awareness of deaf travelers.

Mobility International USA (Box 10767, Eugene, OR 97440; phone 541/343-1284 or visit *www.miusa.org*). Provides referrals for travelers with disabilities as well as doing consultations with groups and exchanges of ideas.

Travel Companions/Travel Care Companions (6965 El Camino Real #105, Carlsbad, CA 92009; phone 800/555-2977, fax 858/481-9182, e-mail *info@travelcarecompanions.com* or visit *www.travelcarecompanions.com*). Matches disabled travelers with international travel companions or caregivers. *ITN*

Travel for the handicapped

I am writing in response to the request for information on traveling by the handicapped (*May '00, pg. 4*). This information is based on my experi-

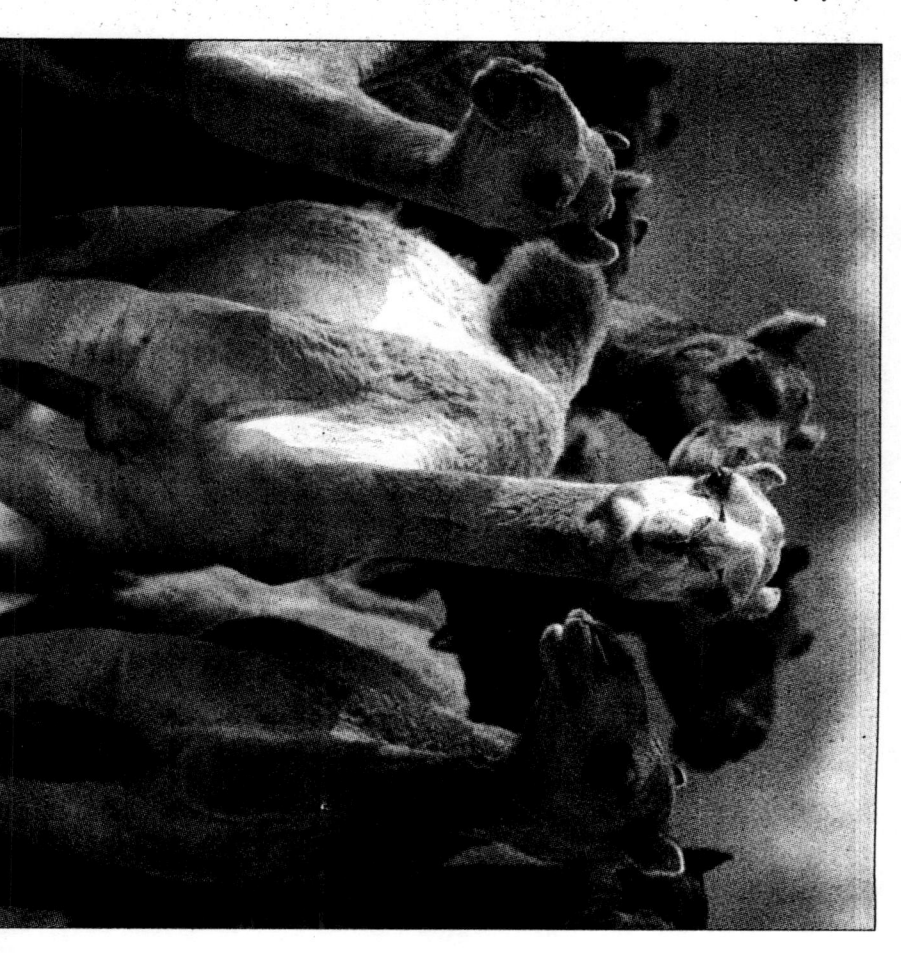